ANTIBIOTICS

Medical
Marvels

ANTIBIOTICS

by Christine Zuchora-Walske

Content Consultant

Erika Ernst
Associate Professor
University of Iowa College of Pharmacy

Credits

Published by ABDO Publishing Company, PO Box 398166, Minneapolis, MN 55439. Copyright © 2014 by Abdo Consulting Group, Inc. International copyrights reserved in all countries. No part of this book may be reproduced in any form without written permission from the publisher. The Essential Library™ is a trademark and logo of ABDO Publishing Company.

Printed in the United States of America,
North Mankato, Minnesota
062013
092013

 THIS BOOK CONTAINS AT LEAST 10% RECYCLED MATERIALS.

Editor: Melissa York
Series Designer: Craig Hinton

Library of Congress Control Number: 2013932973
Cataloging-in-Publication Data

Zuchora-Walske, Christine.
 Antibiotics / Christine Zuchora-Walske.
  p. cm. -- (Medical marvels)
Includes bibliographical references and index.
ISBN 978-1-61783-901-6
1. Antibiotics--Juvenile literature. I. Title.
615/.329--dc23

2013932973

Contents

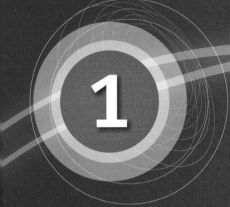

1

Back from the Brink

Albert Alexander was a 43-year-old police constable from Oxford County, England. On a September day in 1940, he had the day off. He chose to spend it working in his rose garden. That simple choice turned out to be a fateful one—both for Alexander himself and for the world. While tending his rosebushes, Constable Alexander suffered a scratch on his face. It seemed to be a minor injury. But bacteria found their way into the scratch, causing an infection. In 1940, an infection was a much bigger problem than it is today.

Back then, doctors had few infection-fighting tools. They knew infections were caused by bacteria and other microbes. Doctors knew keeping wounds and medical supplies as clean as possible could help prevent infection. And they had some antiseptics and cleaning chemicals to do those jobs.

Doctors would soon unlock the antibiotic power of penicillin mold, shown here magnified 2,300 times.

Antibiotics versus Antimicrobials

An antibiotic is any substance produced by a microbe that acts against another microbe. By the strictest definition, antibiotics do not include substances that are synthetic (man-made), partially synthetic, or those that come from plants or animals.

However, many people—including some scientists—use the word *antibiotic* more broadly for any antimicrobial. An antimicrobial is any natural, partially synthetic, or fully synthetic substance that kills or hinders the growth of microbes.

They also had sulfa drugs, which could sometimes slow or stop bacterial growth in people who already had infections. But modern antibiotics weren't available.

Over the next couple of weeks, Alexander's infection spread to his eyes and scalp. He felt—and looked—terrible. By October, he'd checked into the city of Oxford's Radcliffe Infirmary.

Pathetically Ill

Alexander landed in Radcliffe's septic ward. In the days before antibiotics, all hospitals had septic wards. They were for patients who had raging infections—and they were not for the faint of heart. Septic wards were full of feverish people suffering with pain and oozing pus. But misery and gruesomeness weren't the worst aspects of a septic ward. Hopelessness was. According to Charles Fletcher, a young doctor at Radcliffe in the 1940s, medical treatments in septic wards amounted to "bandaging and rest. There was nothing else. About half the people who came to these wards died."[1]

At Radcliffe, Alexander received the best available treatment for his infection. Infirmary staff drained his abscesses and dosed him with sulfa drugs. But the best available treatment simply wasn't good enough. The drugs not only failed but also gave him a rash. And his infection kept spreading.

By February 1941, the infection had destroyed his left eye. Surgeons had to remove it. During the week after that operation, the infection spread to Alexander's shoulder and lungs. He was in terrible pain and was oozing pus from the chest up. "He was . . . desperately and pathetically ill," said Fletcher.[2] Indeed, Alexander seemed very near death.

Human Guinea Pig

But he was not as close to death as he seemed. Alexander had become a patient in Radcliffe's septic ward at a pivotal moment in medical research.

In late 1939, Oxford scientists Howard Florey, Norman Heatley, and Ernst Chain had begun trying to develop a new drug to fight bacterial infections. Earlier research had shown that a mold called penicillium produced a bacteria-killing substance. Florey, Heatley, and Chain spent more than a year growing large amounts of penicillium mold and then extracting and purifying the bactericidal

Identifying Penicillin

People have known about the antibacterial properties of mold since ancient times, but it was Scottish bacteriologist Alexander Fleming who identified penicillin in 1928. Fleming tried for several years to get scientists interested in developing a drug, and he had just given up when the Oxford team began its work.

substance, which they called penicillin. In early 1941, they finally had enough penicillin to test on a human.

First they needed to find out whether penicillin was toxic to humans in general. A test case proved it wasn't. Then they needed to try it on a person who had a bad bacterial infection that hadn't responded to any other treatment. They chose Alexander.

On February 12, 1941, Alexander received 200 milligrams of penicillin intravenously. Every three hours for the next 24 hours, he got another 300-milligram dose.[3] By the next day, some of his abscesses had stopped oozing, and others were slowing down. His fever disappeared, and his appetite returned.

Alexander continued the treatment for five days, until the penicillin ran out. By that time, his facial swelling was almost gone, and his right eye was healing. As

February wore on, he stayed stable. He'd come back from the brink of death. And it looked as if he would recover completely.

Alexander, no doubt, was relieved. The scientists, for their part, were thrilled. Fletcher later recalled "[Dr.] Chain dancing with excitement" and Florey displaying "the intense joy of the scientist seeing that years of work had resulted in an opportunity to save lives."[4]

A Hard Lesson

Because Alexander had improved so dramatically and stayed stable for several days, the Radcliffe team assumed he was cured. There was just one problem. He had not gotten quite enough penicillin to wipe out all the bacteria infecting him.

The First Human Test: Elva Akers

Elva Akers was the first human to get an injection of penicillin. She was 50 years old and had inoperable breast cancer. Although she had only a month or two to live, she had no infection and was not yet at death's door. Giving her penicillin would show whether it was toxic to humans. If she became ill or died soon after the injection, scientists would know penicillin was to blame.

Charles Fletcher explained the situation to Akers, including the potential benefits to humankind and the risks to herself. Then he asked if she would agree to a test injection of penicillin. She readily and proudly did.

After one injection, Akers began shaking and spiked a fever. These symptoms turned out to be from contaminants in the penicillin. Further purification removed them, and a second injection caused no reaction. Akers had proven penicillin was safe for humans.

On February 27, Alexander's infection flared up again, especially in his lungs. The bacteria then invaded his bloodstream. He was sicker than ever. But the doctors had no penicillin to give him.

Infirmary staff had collected all of Alexander's urine. Fletcher had carried it by bicycle to Florey, Heatley, and Chain's laboratory, where the scientists carefully extracted the residual penicillin. But—believing Alexander was cured—they'd already given that penicillin to another patient.

On March 15, Alexander died. His death deeply upset his caregivers, but they took pains to learn from it. First, Florey noted that Alexander's case had proven people could take penicillin for five days with no toxic effects. Later—and more important—Florey reflected that this case had shown five days wasn't enough. Instead of stopping Alexander's treatment as soon as his condition improved, his team should have continued the treatment until all signs of infection were gone.

After Alexander

After the heartbreaking case of Albert Alexander, the Oxford scientists began testing penicillin treatments on sick children. Children's smaller bodies needed smaller amounts of penicillin. Florey, Heatley, and Chain could more easily provide what these children needed, especially as their methods improved.

Howard Florey was one of the doctors who was instrumental in the first penicillin trials.

A US military medical technician prepares antibiotics for injection. Today, we rely on effective and readily available antibiotics to cure illness.

The team of scientists soon demonstrated the effectiveness and safety of penicillin as a drug. Thus began the age of antibiotics. For the first time in human history, people had a powerful tool against bacterial infections, which had once been very dangerous and often deadly. Other scientists developed new antibiotics in the late 1940s. These were followed by many more from the 1950s through the 1970s. Development continued after the 1970s at a slower pace. Today, more than 150 antibiotics in 17 different classes exist.[5]

But modern scientists worry the golden age of antibiotics may be coming to an end. As soon as people began using antibiotic drugs, bacteria began developing resistance to them. All antibiotics currently in use have spawned new strains of bacteria that don't respond to them.

Deadly Infections

Before penicillin, bacterial infections were extremely dangerous and often deadly. For example, approximately half of the soldiers killed in World War I (1914–1918) died not from bullets, gas, bombs, or shrapnel but from infections in relatively minor wounds.[6]

Who will ultimately win this battle? It might be microbes, which have an uncanny ability to evolve and evade the tools meant to kill them. Humans, with their ingenuity and ever-more-powerful antibiotics, are hoping for a different outcome. But only time will tell.

2

Early Antimicrobials

Antibiotic drugs are less than a century old. But the struggle between humans and microbes has been going on for as long as they have lived together on Earth.

Antimicrobials in Ancient Times

Human understanding of infectious disease has come a long way in the last few millennia. Three thousand years ago, humans did not even know microbes existed. They could not see the tiny creatures—and they certainly did not know microbes cause infections.

But the ancients were neither stupid nor helpless. Naturally, people were concerned about the sicknesses that plagued them. They studied the stages of illness and the patterns of contagion.

Long before people understood microbes, they observed symptoms and cured illness.

They aided the sick as best as they could. They noted the treatments that seemed to help. And despite the limitations of primitive medical knowledge and tools, people figured out ways to fight their microscopic foes.

One of the first things ancient healers figured out was that sickness could spread from person to person not only by physical contact but also by sharing items such as clothing and household tools. This knowledge appears in the book of Leviticus, a part of the Jewish-Christian Bible written down between the 1100s and 400s BCE. Chapter 13 of Leviticus details how to determine whether a person's skin rash is leprosy, a bacterial infection known today as Hansen's disease. It also explains how community leaders should isolate an infected person to avoid spreading the disease to others: "All the days during which he has the infection . . . he shall live alone; his dwelling shall be outside the camp."[1]

Another important idea humans figured out thousands of years ago was that some natural substances could ward off—or help heal—infectious diseases. Scientists have found evidence that not long after the time of Leviticus, civilizations in northern Africa, the Middle East, and China were all using such substances.

Tetracycline is an antibiotic substance discovered in the 1940s and developed into a drug in the 1950s. In the 1980s, a researcher accidentally discovered tetracycline in a bone of a mummy from Nubia in modern-day northern Sudan dating to the 300s CE. After this surprising discovery, scientists examined

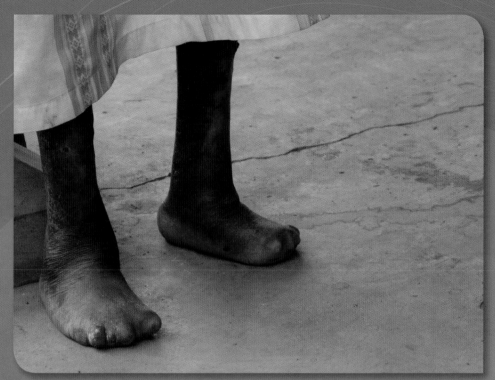

+ Hansen's Disease

Hansen's disease causes skin sores, nerve damage, and muscle weakness. Symptoms get worse over time. People suffering Hansen's disease can eventually lose digits through infection. The disease is caused by the bacterium *Mycobacterium leprae*. It is not very contagious, but it is common in many countries worldwide. The United States has approximately 100 cases per year.[2] Effective antibiotic medications exist to treat Hansen's disease, and isolating patients is no longer necessary.

bones from more than 100 individuals who had lived in ancient Nubia, Egypt, and Jordan from the 100s BCE to approximately 500 CE. They found tetracycline in all but four of the individuals. The pattern of bone deposits showed the people had ingested tetracycline while they were alive; the substance had not somehow gotten into their bones after burial. Further research revealed the source of this tetracycline was beer.

+ A Happy Accident

In 1980, Debra Martin was a graduate student in biological anthropology. Biological anthropology is the study of humans' physical development as a species. At a research lab in Detroit, Michigan, Martin was learning how to make thin sections of mummy bones for study under a microscope.

The standard microscopes were all in use. So she tried one that emitted ultraviolet light instead. Ultraviolet light is invisible to the human eye. This led to a happy accident. Martin saw the bone glowing yellow-green under the ultraviolet microscope. In ultraviolet light, tetracycline fluoresces with a unique yellow-green color. When Martin saw this color, she knew what it meant. She was startled and excited to find something so unexpected—a modern antibiotic in an ancient body.

In this part of the ancient world, a nutritious, soup-like beer was a dietary staple. This beer was also the perfect breeding ground for streptomycetes, which are mold-like bacteria that produce tetracycline. The ancients knew their beer was good for their health, even if they didn't know exactly why. A large body of archaeological and historical evidence shows Egyptians and their neighbors using beer in wound dressings, as a mouthwash to treat the gums, and in other medicinal ways. This widespread use of beer did, in fact, seem to ward off sickness. The Nubian nation survived for a long time, into the 1300s CE. And the rate of infectious diseases recorded in the Sudanese Nubian population was low.

Another early antibiotic example is the medical use of soil in Jordan. Both historical records and recent anecdotes from Jordan tell stories about people curing skin infections by applying a particular type of red soil found there. When scientists examined this soil, they found it contained a variety of antibiotic-producing bacteria.

Indeed, traditional medical practices around the world provide many examples of early antibiotic use. The ancient Egyptians used moldy bread to treat skin lesions. The ancient Chinese put a different twist on that treatment: they applied moldy tofu to infected and inflamed skin. Chinese herbalists have used the plant artemisia, also called sweet wormwood, as a remedy for many illnesses since at least as early as 168 BCE. Modern scientists studying this herb have discovered it to be an effective treatment for malaria, a disease caused by microbes called protozoans.

Understanding Microbes

Although the ancients had some weapons that worked against disease-causing microbes, people didn't actually

Odd but Effective

Before antibiotic drugs were invented, humans benefited from natural antibiotic substances in a number of odd—but effective—ways. In 1640, for instance, English apothecary John Parkinson recommended using mold "taken from the sculles [skulls] of those that have been hanged or executed for offences."[3] And historical records show ancient people in Mesopotamia and Egypt ate dirt to treat ailments of the gut. In fact, geophagia, the practice of eating earth for health reasons, is common in modern non-Western cultures around the world.

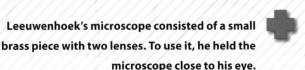

know about microbes until the 1600s CE. Antonie van Leeuwenhoek was the one who revealed them.

Leeuwenhoek was a Dutch textile merchant and maker of glass lenses. He did not invent the microscope, but he did improve it dramatically. In the 1670s, using his own homemade microscopes, Leeuwenhoek saw "many thousands of living creatures in one small drop of water, all huddling and moving, but each creature having its own motion."[4] He was surprised and delighted by the creatures, which he called "animalcules."[5] They were, in fact, bacteria and other microbes—and he was the first human to see them. At first, other scientists ridiculed him. They did not believe objects so small could possibly be living creatures, and they said Leeuwenhoek was telling fairy tales.

The scientific community eventually admitted microbes existed. But it took another 200 years for humans to figure

Leeuwenhoek's Microscopes

Leeuwenhoek made a microscope for every specimen he studied and wrote about, leaving behind 247 complete microscopes, most containing specimens, plus 172 additional lenses.[6] He explained why: "Whenever I make any Discovery, which I apprehend will not easily meet with Credit, I suffer the Object to lie before the Microscope Day after Day, and sometimes for whole Years together . . . to let it be seen by as many different Persons as possible."[7]

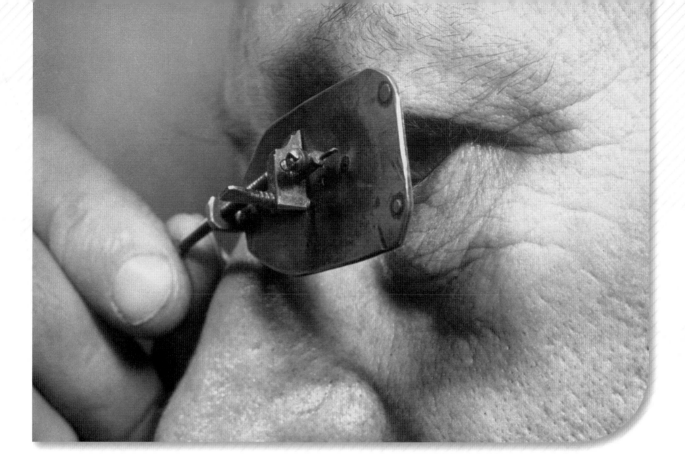

out what those tiny creatures did. Throughout the 1700s and 1800s, scientists inched closer to an answer. They developed the germ theory of disease in the mid-1800s. But this idea was controversial. Eventually, experiments by French scientist Louis Pasteur and German scientist Robert Koch in the late 1800s proved the germ theory. By the end of the century, scientists had identified the microbes responsible for many diseases in humans and animals.

The Discovery of Synthetic Antimicrobials

Once the scientific community began understanding microbes, it was only a matter of time before it began trying to stop the dangerous ones. In the early 1900s, German scientist Paul Ehrlich noticed certain synthetic dyes could stain specific microbes but not others. Based on this observation, Ehrlich believed people could come up with similarly selective drugs. Such medicinal "magic bullets" would target only disease-causing microbes without damaging the microbes' host.[8]

Ehrlich was determined to find one of these magic bullets for syphilis. Syphilis is a sexually transmitted disease caused by the bacterium *Treponema pallidum*. At this time, syphilis was widespread and nearly incurable. It had been a major international public health problem since it leapt from the New World to the Old with Christopher Columbus's voyages. The only available treatment, which contained mercury, often didn't work, and it caused severe side effects. So Ehrlich started systematically testing hundreds of arsenicals against syphilis. Arsenicals are compounds that contain

Syphilis begins with genital sores and then progresses to a general rash. Soon, disfiguring abscesses and scabs appear all over the body. Untreated late-stage syphilis can cause heart abnormalities, mental disorders, blindness, other neurological problems, and death.

the element arsenic. They were used to treat a wide variety of diseases at that time. Ehrlich instructed his staff to study these compounds to find one that had maximum effect on the bacterium with minimal effect on human tissues.

In 1909, Ehrlich hit the jackpot. Compound number 606 cured syphilis in rabbits. Human testing in 1910 showed promise, too. Ehrlich used these results to develop the drug Salvarsan and an improved version called Neosalvarsan. Salvarsan means "that which saves by arsenic."[9] For the next three decades, these two drugs were the most frequently prescribed drugs in the world.[10]

Other scientists learned Ehrlich's method of systematically screening chemicals for possible use as drugs. In the 1930s, chemists at the Bayer pharmaceutical company in Germany and at the Pasteur Institute in France used this approach. They learned the compound

Mercury and Arsenic

Mercury, a silvery liquid metal, has intrigued humans since ancient times. The ancient Greeks, Romans, Chinese, and Hindus each had their own legends about mercury. All believed mercury was powerful and possibly magical. At the same time, people knew it was poisonous. It was obvious workers who mined mercury ore became sick—first with tremors, then with severe mental impairment. Modern medicine does not use mercury because it is so toxic to humans. Its use in industry is limited because it might leak into the environment.

Arsenic is a mineral that occurs naturally in rock, soil, water, air, plants, and animals. Humans have known it is poisonous for centuries. In fact, from the Middle Ages to the mid-1800s, arsenic was a popular murder tool because it was readily available and undetectable. Arsenic is odorless and tasteless. Symptoms of arsenic poisoning include nausea, vomiting, diarrhea, and abdominal pain—all of which can be blamed easily on common diseases. And until 1836, no method existed for measuring arsenic in organisms or substances.

sulfanilamide, used in a synthetic dye called Prontosil, could slow bacterial growth in mammals. This discovery led to the development of a wide variety of sulfa drugs. Sulfa drugs were the first synthetic antimicrobial drugs.

Neither Salvarsan nor sulfanilamide was the magic bullet scientists had been looking for, though. Salvarsan treatment had to be given intravenously over a period of at least 18 months. It was a long, unpleasant affair that often caused miserable nausea and vomiting. Sulfanilamide had its drawbacks, too. It worked against only one kind of bacteria, streptococcus. Streptococcus bacteria cause skin infections, the serious lung infection pneumonia, and meningitis (an infection of the meninges, or membranes covering the brain and spinal cord). And sulfanilamide didn't work at all in infections that were producing pus. Also, negative reactions to sulfanilamide, such as rashes, light sensitivity, and fever, were common.

The medical community made the most of these pharmaceutical achievements. But behind the scenes, scientists continued searching for better weapons against infection. During this time, Alexander Fleming appeared on the scene. In 1900, Fleming was a lowly 19-year-old clerk for a London shipping company. But that would soon change.

Paul Ehrlich studied blood, infections, and immunity, in addition to his work on syphilis.

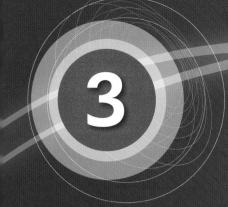

3

Penicillin

Alexander Fleming was born in 1881 on a farm in Scotland. He was the seventh of eight children. His oldest brother inherited the farm when their father died. One by one, the other siblings moved to London. In 1895, Alexander joined them. He lived with his older brother Thomas, who was a doctor. Thomas, who had trouble establishing his practice, advised Alexander to study commerce. So Alexander did, and within two years, he landed a job as a clerk for the America Line shipping company.

Fleming did not like the work, though; he found it terribly boring. In 1900, he inherited some money from an uncle. He used it to pay for medical school. By 1906, he had finished his studies and joined the bacteriology lab at the prestigious Saint Mary's Inoculation Department.

Although Alexander Fleming performed many experiments in his pursuit of an antimicrobial substance, he discovered penicillin by accident.

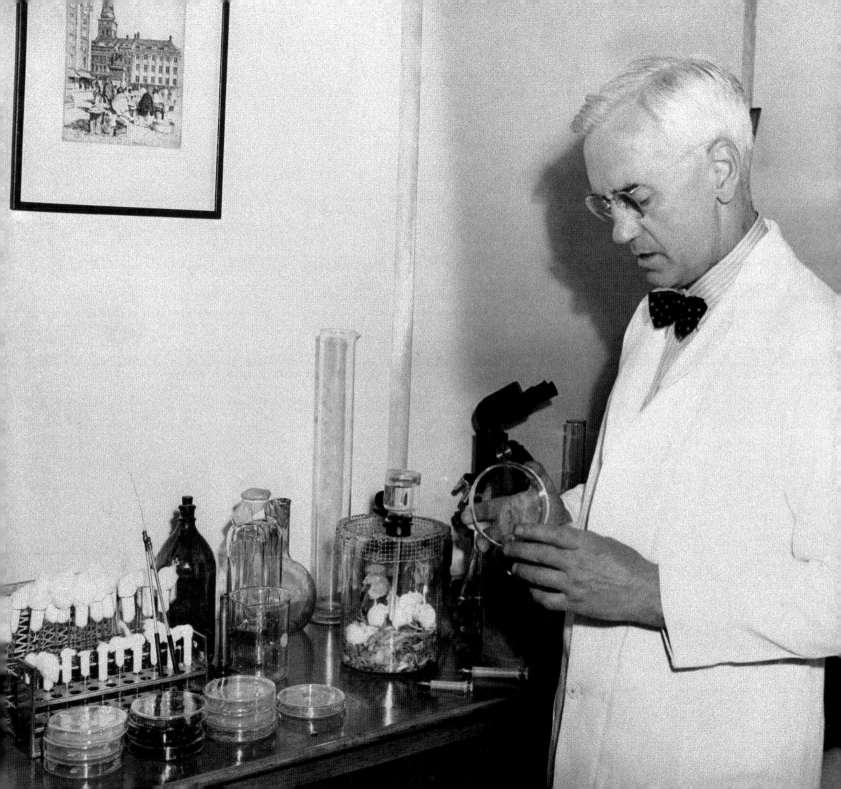

Fleming's Makeshift Lab

Fleming's laboratory in Boulogne, France, was a former fencing practice room in the attic of a casino. He used his own ingenuity to outfit it. He brought in water by jury-rigging gas cans and pumps. He used paraffin stoves to make incubators for growing microbes. He made his own glass lab equipment by using a burner powered with a foot bellows. He tweaked Bunsen burners, which usually burn gas, so they could burn alcohol—which was more available—instead.

Later, Fleming remarked that this makeshift lab was the best he'd ever worked in. He hated fancy, overly equipped laboratories. He believed that a fancy lab tempted researchers to spend all their time playing with the equipment instead of conducting experiments.

When World War I broke out in 1914, Fleming went to France with a team from Saint Mary's. The team's job was figuring out how to better control wound infections, which were killing soldiers by the thousands. In a makeshift attic lab, Fleming examined and experimented with specimens from soldiers' wounds, dressings, and clothing, as well as the soil on which wounded soldiers lay. He realized the antiseptic dressings commonly used on war wounds were no match for the teeming bacteria in the soil and clothing that covered soldiers and infected their raggedly torn flesh.

Fleming felt there must be some treatment that could overcome microbial infections even in the severe wounds of war. After the war, he returned to London and turned his focus in that direction. Throughout the 1920s, he searched high and low for such a treatment. He found it by accident, in a place where he wasn't even looking.

Fleming's Discovery of Penicillin

Fleming once described his work by saying, "I play with microbes."[1] His playful attitude was evident in the state of his lab, which was often a jumbled mess. Modern scientists would likely be appalled at Fleming's mess. But the truth is, if he had been tidier, he probably would not have stumbled on penicillin.

In the fall of 1928, he was straightening up a sink full of petri dishes in which he had been growing bacteria. He examined each dish before tossing it into a cleaning solution. One made him stop and look more closely. Some mold was growing in the dish—which was not surprising, considering the mess. What was surprising was that all around the mold, the bacteria had died. These bacteria were staphylococci—microbes that cause skin and blood infections—against which sulfanilamide had no effect.

Fleming took a sample of the mold so he could study it. He soon identified the mold as penicillium. He discovered it was secreting a bacteria-killing substance. He called this substance penicillin.

Fleming wasn't the first scientist to notice that penicillium mold could kill bacteria. But he was the first one to stop and investigate this phenomenon. He soon found penicillin could kill more than one group of harmful bacteria—not only staphylococci, but also streptococci, meningococci (bacteria that cause meningitis), and diphtheria bacteria. Diphtheria is a contagious disease that causes fever, sore

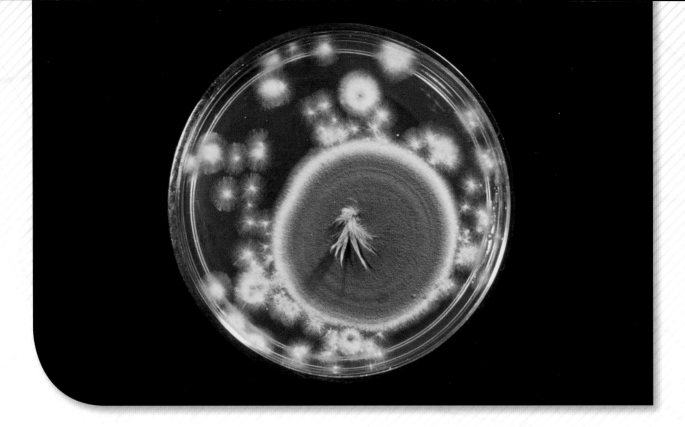

throat, and swollen glands in the neck. In 1929, he published an article on his penicillin discoveries in a scholarly journal.

Fleming spent the next several years studying the mold and trying to grow and refine penicillin. But he was a bacteriologist, not a mold specialist or a chemist, and he had trouble assembling a team to help him. The scientific community simply was not very interested in his work. Fleming gave up his penicillin efforts in 1935. It took another world war to get people interested in penicillin again.

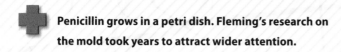

Penicillin grows in a petri dish. Fleming's research on the mold took years to attract wider attention.

The Oxford Team

In 1938, Howard Florey was the director of Oxford University's Dunn School of Pathology. He had hired biochemists Ernst Chain and Norman Heatley to serve as researchers and professors there. The men were looking for an unexplored field of research in which to make their mark. They agreed antibacterial substances offered them the perfect opportunity.

Chain gathered 200 reports on substances scientists had found that hindered the growth of bacteria. He read each carefully. One was Fleming's 1929 article, "On the Antibacterial Action of Cultures of a Penicillium." When Chain read it, he was "immediately interested."[2] So was Florey.

By the end of 1938, Nazi Germany was armed to the teeth and threatening all its neighbors. The United Kingdom was still working for peace, but the country started bracing for war. In January 1939, Florey requested funding to explore the nature of penicillin. He insisted penicillin's potential as a drug—one that might be very useful during

Florey had read Fleming's article long before 1938; in fact, he was the editor who accepted it for publication in the *British Journal of Experimental Pathology* in 1929. But he failed to remember it, even after Chain pointed it out.

war, at that—was not his motivation; rather, it was pure scientific inquiry that interested him. But his own writings suggest otherwise. In an earlier letter to his wife, Florey had described his distress over untreatable infections as "the appalling thing of seeing young people maimed or wiped out while one can do nothing."[3]

The Rockefeller Foundation, a philanthropic organization in the United States, responded to Florey's request with a generous grant. With the sheer size of its grant, the foundation made it clear that it, too, believed penicillin research was very important. The Oxford team was off and running.

Bedpans, Butter Churns, and Bathtubs

War may have been a motivator for penicillin research, but it also added challenges to the process. Everything was in short supply, including lab materials. The team needed to produce approximately 130 gallons (500 L) of "mold juice" per week in order to carry out a series of animal experiments with penicillin. That meant they needed a lot of containers for growing mold.

Heatley was in charge of this part of the process. Undeterred by supply shortages, he simply used whatever he could find that worked. This turned out to be an array of bedpans, butter churns, and bathtubs all rigged together.

Chain was in charge of finding a way to extract penicillin from the mold juice. Penicillin was very unstable; when separated from the mold juice, it tended to evaporate or lose its antibacterial quality. Chain struggled for months with this problem. Eventually, in spring 1940, Heatley came up with a solution. His method for extracting penicillin from the mold juice used a crazy-looking contraption made of a cast-off bookcase, homemade glass tubing, pumps, laboratory bottles, an old doorbell, colored lights, nozzles, and homemade copper coils.

By May 1940, the team had enough penicillin to test on mice. First they infected eight mice with lethal doses of streptococci bacteria. Then they injected four of the mice with penicillin. In the morning, the untreated mice were dead. Those that had received penicillin, however,

The Secret of the Moldy Clothes

The Oxford team knew how valuable their penicillin work was to their country. They also knew how valuable it could be to Nazi Germany, their enemy in World War II (1939–1945). The Nazis might invade at any time, so the scientists needed a plan to keep their work out of enemy hands. They'd probably have only a few hours' notice to destroy their work, salvage a bit of penicillium mold, and escape. They came up with a plan that was simple, quick, and clever. If necessary, they would rub mold spores all over their clothes to carry them to safety. Spores are tiny, tough reproductive particles; they can lie inactive for years until revived by the proper conditions. And nobody would be able to detect them.

survived. They continued testing more and more mice, varying the amounts of bacteria and penicillin, with continually positive results.

The scientists were thrilled. As Duncan Gardner, a member of the team, recalled, "There could be no further doubt that penicillin was the very thing that doctors for a century had hoped and longed for."[4]

But the results were sobering, too. Success in mice meant the team would eventually need to test penicillin in humans. Humans are approximately 3,000 times larger than mice. To conduct human trials,

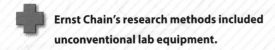
Ernst Chain's research methods included unconventional lab equipment.

the team would need to produce 3,000 times more penicillin than it was already producing. That was a daunting task.

To accomplish the task of producing, extracting, and purifying enough penicillin to test in humans, the team turned the Dunn School into a 24-hour penicillin factory. Bedpans had proven to be the most efficient vessels for producing mold juice. But there weren't enough bedpans to spare at Oxford's Radcliffe Infirmary. So Heatley drew some sketches and found a local ceramics factory willing to make 700 of them for a reasonable price.[5]

Once the team had arranged the vessels to create a penicillin production line, they realized they would need some help to keep the line going. Almost every eligible young man in Oxford—scholar or otherwise—was going off to war, so the team hired six young women instead.

The Overlooked Genius

For discovering and developing penicillin as a drug, Alexander Fleming, Howard Florey, and Ernst Chain shared the 1945 Nobel Prize in Physiology or Medicine. Norman Heatley was never considered for it—most likely because his work in developing penicillin was of such a practical nature, according to Henry Harris, a colleague at the Dunn School.

Heatley was a versatile, clever, and skilled laboratory engineer. He was not only a biochemist but also an expert in optics, glassmaking, metalworking, plumbing, carpentry, and electricity. He provided what Florey and Chain lacked: the technical expertise needed to produce penicillin. Harris insists "without Heatley, [there would be] no penicillin."[6]

This crew of research assistants became known as the Penicillin Girls.

By early 1941, the team had at last produced enough penicillin to test on a human. Cancer patient Elva Akers helped them prove that penicillin was not toxic to humans. Next, septic patient Albert Alexander helped them show that penicillin could successfully treat a bacterial infection in humans.

Pharmaceutical Penicillin

Several more human trials produced similarly impressive results. Soon the British government was making plans to provide penicillin to British troops on the battlefields of World War II.

Pharmaceutical companies—first in the United States and then in the United Kingdom—began manufacturing penicillin. Meanwhile, large clinical studies confirmed

Penicillin Girls

The Penicillin Girls were, in fact, women as young as 16: Ruth Callow Parker, Claire Inayat, Megan Lancaster, Betty Cooke, Peggy Gardner, and Patricia McKegney. They worked six days a week, sometimes seven, washing, filling, emptying, and monitoring the vessels in the penicillin production line. Sometimes when the Germans were bombing they stood guard through the night, watching for fire. Though they were young, they knew their work was important. Parker later recalled "a sense of how special that time was."[7]

penicillin's promise as an infection-fighting drug. It was effective against multiple bacteria, including streptococci, staphylococci, gonococci (the bacteria that cause gonorrhea, a sexually transmitted disease), and treponema (the bacteria that cause syphilis).

By 1944, penicillin had become the primary treatment for syphilis in the British and American armed forces. Penicillin accompanied the troops in June 1944, and it dramatically reduced their death toll from infected wounds when they stormed the beaches at Normandy, France, during the D-day attack.

Antibiotic Explosion

The discovery, development, and success of penicillin inspired renewed efforts to find and develop other antibiotic drugs. These efforts bore great fruit. Beginning in the mid-1940s, a variety of new antibiotics appeared on the scene. The period from the mid-1940s to 1970 was the golden era of new antibiotic discovery. Scientists have continued to discover and introduce new antimicrobial compounds since 1970, but their progress has slowed dramatically.

Drugs from Dirt

Almost immediately after penicillin's debut, scientist Selman Waksman discovered another important antibiotic. For several decades, Waksman had been studying and experimenting with soil bacteria. He and other soil microbiologists had noticed that despite the massive amount of animal waste in

Continued study of bacteria found many new antibacterial substances—even bacteria that kill other bacteria.

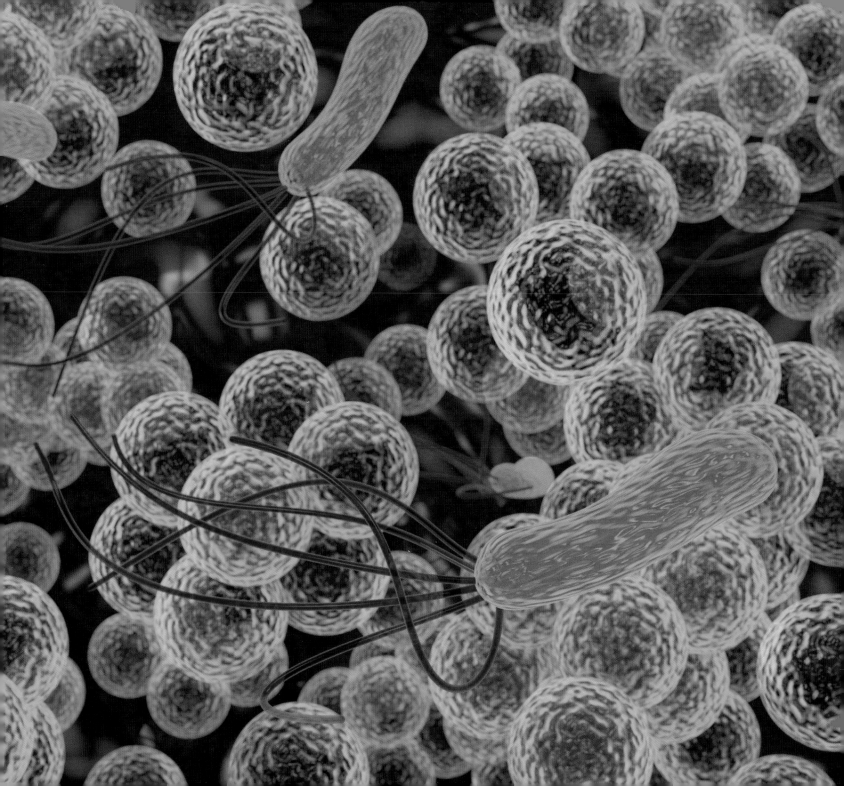

soil, "soil harbors . . . few bacteria capable of causing infectious diseases."[1] They realized some biological interaction must be happening in the soil, and they wanted to find out what it was.

In 1939, one of Waksman's former students, René Dubos, had identified a soil bacterium, *Bacillus brevis*, that produced a substance able to kill staphylococci and other infectious bacteria. Dubos called this substance gramicidin. Unfortunately, though, gramicidin was too toxic for humans to take internally.

After Dubos's discovery, Waksman was determined to find more antibiotic substances in soil. From more than 10,000 candidates, he chose ten promising soil microorganisms to study.[2] In 1943, a

graduate student working with him, Albert Schatz, discovered that one of these bacteria, *Streptomyces griseus*, produced a substance that could kill bacteria responsible for a wide variety of common infections. These included urinary tract infections, meningitis, tularemia (a tick-borne disease), and tuberculosis (an often-fatal lung disease). The substance, which Waksman called streptomycin, was the first effective remedy for tuberculosis.

Streptomycin did have serious potential side effects, however. It occasionally caused kidney damage or deafness. An effort to find similar but safer antibiotics spawned the development of an entire family of antibiotic drugs called aminoglycosides. This family includes streptomycin, neomycin (1949), kanamycin (1957), gentamicin (1963), tobramycin (1971), and amikacin (1976).

Experiment Eleven

Waksman alone received public credit for the discovery of streptomycin, as well as the 1952 Nobel Prize in Physiology or Medicine for this achievement. However, archival records at Rutgers University, where Waksman and Schatz worked together, tell a different story.

In Schatz's lab notebook, his August 23, 1943, entry describes what he called Experiment Eleven. It explains that he found antibiotic-producing soil microbes in "leaf compost, straw compost, and stable manure" on the farm outside his lab.[3] And it details his experiments with the microbes and his discovery that *Streptomyces griseus* could destroy tuberculosis bacteria and *E. coli*, a bacterium that causes urinary tract infections and food poisoning.

Broad-Spectrum Antibiotics

In 1947, microbiologist Paul Burkholder discovered a new soil bacterium. The bacterium produced a substance capable of killing a wide variety of bacteria types, not just one or a few kinds of bacteria. A substance with this ability is a broad-spectrum antibiotic.

This soil bacteria, now called *Streptomyces venezuelae*, produced a compound called chloramphenicol. It was the first broad-spectrum antibiotic. Among the bacteria affected by chloramphenicol were those that caused typhus (a disease spread by body lice), Rocky Mountain spotted fever (a dangerous tick-borne disease), typhoid fever (a disease spread by contaminated food or water), cholera (an intestinal infection), pneumonia, and meningitis.

Chloramphenicol was clearly very useful, but it had one dangerous side effect. For approximately one patient in every 40,000, the drug suppressed bone marrow, the tissue inside bones that produces new blood cells.[4] This sometimes led to aplastic anemia (a fatal condition in which bone marrow does not produce enough new cells to replenish blood cells) and leukemia (cancer of the blood or bone marrow). Although bone marrow suppression is rare, it is so serious doctors decided early on to use chloramphenicol sparingly. And scientists kept looking for other broad-spectrum antibiotics.

It wasn't long before another one surfaced. While Burkholder studied *Streptomyces venezuelae*, Benjamin Duggar was investigating the golden substance produced by the bacterium *Streptomyces*

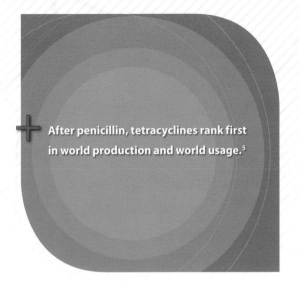

After penicillin, tetracyclines rank first in world production and world usage.[5]

aureofaciens. In 1947, Duggar found that the substance, now known as chlortetracycline, was another effective antibiotic. He discovered it worked against a long list of disease-causing bacteria and fungi. The drug, introduced in 1948, had many side effects in humans, but they were far less severe than those of chloramphenicol. The discovery of chlortetracycline led to the development of a new family of antibiotics called tetracyclines, which includes oxytetracycline (1950), doxycycline (1966), minocycline (1972), tigecycline (2005), and several others.

A Different Path: Antifungals

In the 1940s, many scientists were working feverishly to identify new antibacterial substances. This work inspired microbiologist Elizabeth Hazen and biochemist Rachel Brown to join the search. However, Hazen and Brown took a slightly different path. They knew infections caused by fungi were just as widespread, persistent, and dangerous as those caused by bacteria. In addition, the rise of antibiotics

Fungus among Us

Fungal infections range from the merely annoying to the deadly. Many common skin infections, such as athlete's foot, jock itch, ringworm, and diaper rash, are caused by fungi. So are yeast infections, such as oral thrush and vaginal yeast infections. Fungi are also the culprits behind more serious infections, such as coccidioidomycosis (a lung infection), histoplasmosis (a flu-like sickness), cryptococcal meningitis (fungal meningitis), and candidemia (a blood infection).

was causing a rise in fungal infections. Bacteria are the natural enemies of fungi. When antibiotics kill off bacteria, fungi flourish.

Hazen and Brown were both working for the New York State Department of Health. In New York City, Hazen cultured soil bacteria and tested them for fungicidal activity. She mailed any promising culture to Brown in Albany. Brown isolated the active ingredient and mailed it back to Hazen. Hazen then tested it against two prominent disease-causing fungi. Using this process, in 1950 Hazen and Brown investigated the bacterium *Streptomyces noursei*. They found it produced a powerful fungicide with low toxicity in animals. They named this fungicidal substance nystatin in honor of their employer, the state of New York.

After earning a patent in 1957, nystatin became the first successful antifungal drug. Nystatin opened the door to developing other antifungal antibiotics, such as amphotericin (1957), griseofulvin (1958), azole drugs (multiple types, 1969 to present), caspofungin (2001), and others.

The Story of Cephalosporins

The development of cephalosporin antibiotics followed a long and winding path. The journey started in the 1940s but didn't end with a drug until the 1960s.

Giuseppe Brotzu, a scientist in the city of Cagliari on Italy's island of Sardinia, wondered why typhoid fever was less severe in his city than in other cities. He had also noticed that even though many people swam in the bay where the city's sewer system emptied into the sea, these people did not suffer typhoid outbreaks. Typhoid fever is spread by food or water contaminated with the waste of an infected person. It causes fever, rash, and diarrhea.

So in 1945, Brotzu took a sample of the water and tested its effect on typhoid bacteria. He eventually identified and isolated a fungus, *Acremonium chrysogenum*. The fungus produced a substance capable of killing a wide variety of bacteria, including the one that causes typhoid fever.

Brotzu had no funding for further study. He tried but failed to interest an Italian pharmaceutical company in investing in his work. So he sent a sample of the fungus to the Dunn School at Oxford University. It took many years for the Oxford team to purify the antibiotic substance. Finally, in 1964,

Antiprotozoals

Some microbial infections, such as malaria (a disease that causes high fevers, chills, flu-like symptoms, and anemia), African sleeping sickness (a disease spread by the tsetse fly), and giardiasis (an intestinal infection), are caused by protozoans. Protozoans are single-celled organisms that are more complex than bacteria. They are not animals, but they have some traits, such as the ability to move about, that are typically associated with animals. Protozoan species, like animal species, are very different from one another. By contrast, bacteria species are more similar to one another.

Antiprotozoals are medications that act against protozoans. Each antiprotozoal medication targets a specific species of protozoan. Some antibacterial or antifungal antibiotics, such as tetracycline, also affect some protozoans. Many antiprotozoal medications are not antibiotics by the strictest definition. That is, they are synthetic or semisynthetic substances, or they are substances produced by plants or animals, not microbes.

two broad-spectrum cephalosporin drugs, called cephalothin and cephaloridine, were introduced.

Synthetic Antimicrobials

By the 1950s, some bacteria (especially staphylococci) were already developing resistance to penicillin. Resistant bacteria would no longer respond to penicillin treatment. So the search was on for penicillin-like antibiotics that could fight these resistant bacteria.

Scientists at a British pharmaceutical company took the approach of altering the chemical compounds in penicillin. In 1959, they succeeded in creating a semisynthetic penicillin. They called it methicillin. Over the years, scientists continued to modify penicillin, resulting in different derivatives, or structurally related chemicals. Some derivatives were ampicillin (1961) and amoxicillin (1984).

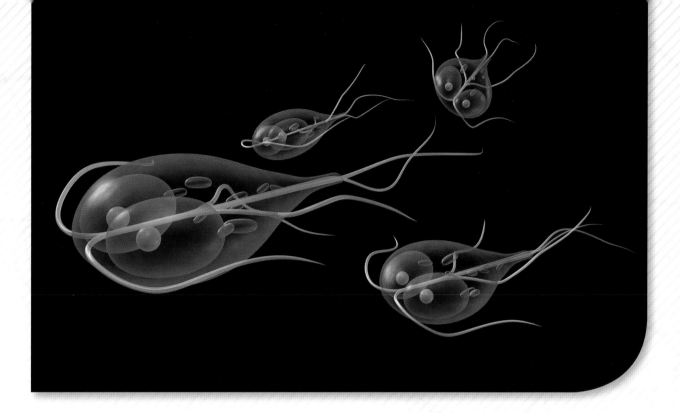

Sulfanilamide, introduced in 1935, was the first synthetic antimicrobial. Many derivative sulfa drugs followed. It would be a long time before another fully synthetic antimicrobial appeared on the scene. Trimethoprim came on the market in the 1970s, and a family of drugs called fluoroquinolones followed more recently. Fluoroquinolones—especially the drug ciprofloxacin, commonly called cipro—showed great promise against hard-to-treat bacterial infections. Cipro was so popular that its sales brought in more than $1 billion per year in the 1990s.[6] But in the 2000s, even fluoroquinolones are growing less and less effective as more and more resistant bacteria develop.

Antibacterial Antibiotics

An antibiotic can be any microbial substance that acts against any other microbe: bacterium, fungus, or protozoan. But when most people talk about antibiotics, they are referring to medicines that fight bacteria. These medicines are antibacterial antibiotics. How do antibacterial antibiotics work? In order to understand that, one must first have some basic knowledge about bacteria.

Bacteria Basics

A bacterium is a tiny organism made up of only one cell. Bacteria are so small it would take approximately 1,000 of them lined up in single file to cross the diameter of an ordinary pencil eraser.[1] They are visible only with a microscope.

Colonies of *Staphylococcus aureus* grow in a petri dish. *S. aureus* can cause skin infections but most strains are not harmful.

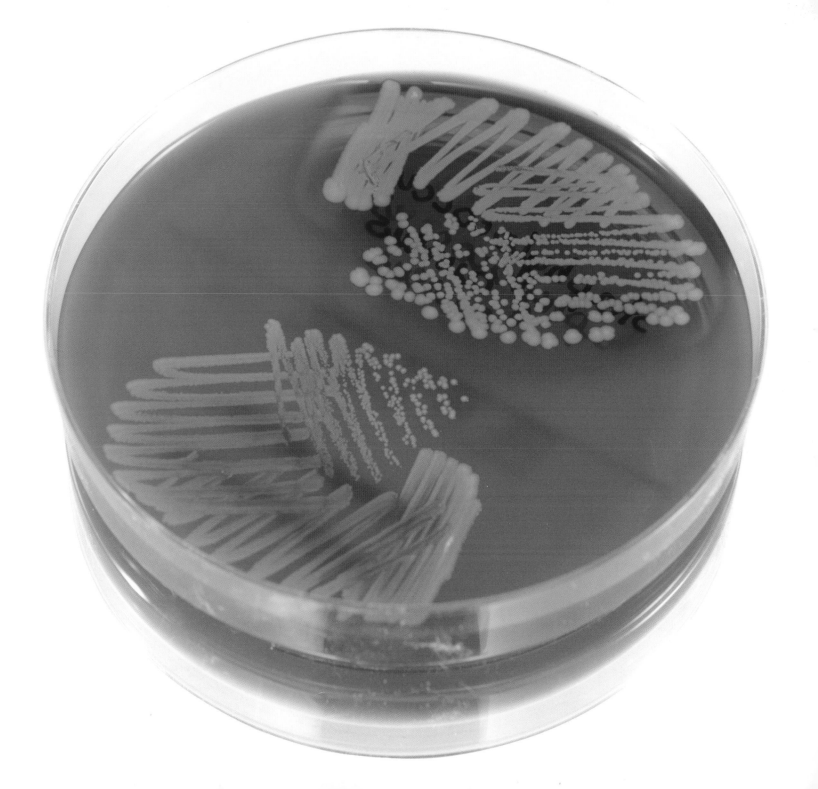

Bacteria can live individually, but they typically live in large groups called colonies. The bacteria in a colony work together to obtain nutrients for growth and survival. The colony competes collectively against other bacteria and against predatory microbes that want to eat the bacteria.

Bacteria reproduce by simple division. That is, they duplicate their cell components and split in half. Bacterial cell division can take anywhere from several hours to several days. Compared with other organisms, bacteria multiply quickly. A colony of bacteria is usually made up of the offspring of one original bacterium.

Scientists classify bacteria in a few ways. One is by shape. Bacteria exist in five basic shapes: sphere, rod, comma, threadlike, and spiral or corkscrew.

Another way in which scientists classify bacteria is by the makeup of their cell walls. Some bacteria have a thick cell wall. When treated with a special dye called Gram's stain, the cell walls of these bacteria hold the dye and appear purple or blue. They are called gram-positive bacteria. Other bacteria have a thinner cell wall. When treated with Gram's stain, these bacteria do not hold the dye and appear red or pink. They are called gram-negative bacteria. Some bacteria cannot be classified by Gram's stain.

Scientists also classify bacteria according to how they function. For example, some bacteria called chemotrophs use chemical compounds as energy sources, while other bacteria called phototrophs use

Gram-positive streptococcus bacteria, *top,* **turn purple when treated with Gram's stain. The bacteria that causes gonorrhea,** *bottom,* **is gram negative.**

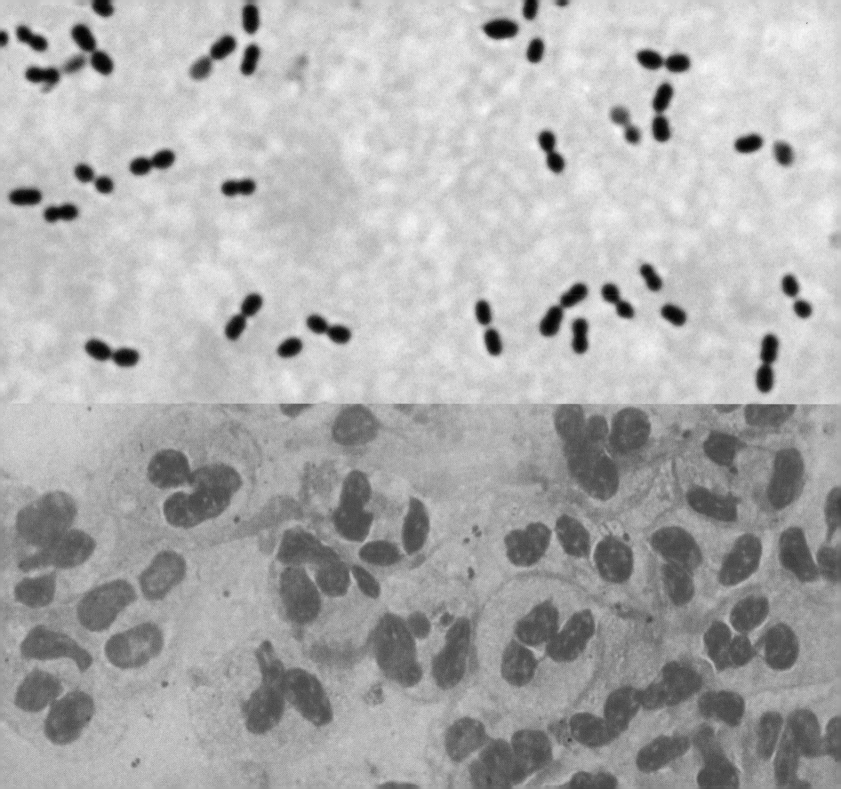

Just How Small Are Bacteria?

Bacteria are visible under an ordinary microscope at a magnification factor of 1,000 times. But even at this enlargement, they look like mere specks. It takes a powerful electron microscope to see the shapes of bacteria clearly. In one milliliter of liquid, 1 million bacteria are invisible. It takes 10 million to 100 million bacteria to make one milliliter of liquid cloudy.[4]

light. Aerobic bacteria need oxygen in order to turn nutrients into energy, while anaerobic bacteria cannot tolerate oxygen. Some bacteria can move about, while others cannot.

"Good" and "Bad" Bacteria

More than 99 percent of all bacteria are helpful.[2] Bacteria that perform useful functions in nature and do not cause disease as they go about their lives are considered "good" bacteria. They are called nonpathogenic bacteria. Bacteria live everywhere in nature. They live on mountaintops, ocean floors, and even in Antarctica's frozen rocks and ice. They live in the intestines of animals and humans, where they help digest food and destroy disease-causing microbes. They live in the soil and help break down dead organisms.

Less than 1 percent of bacteria are harmful.[3] "Bad" bacteria are called pathogenic bacteria. Bacterial infection or disease occurs when pathogenic bacteria enter the body and multiply into large numbers before the body can kill, disable, or remove them. Many of these bacteria produce toxins, or substances that damage the host's tissues and make the host sick. In humans, pathogenic bacteria can cause a wide variety of infections and diseases. These conditions range from the relatively mild, such as strep throat, to the deadly, such as anthrax, which is a lethal infection of the skin, lungs, or intestinal tract.

How Antibiotics Fight Bacteria

The typical treatment for a bacterial infection is a course of medication that contains an antibacterial antibiotic. The appropriate antibiotic depends on the type of bacteria causing the infection.

Different antibiotics have different effects on bacteria. A drug that kills bacteria is called bactericidal. Aminoglycosides, cephalosporins, penicillins, and quinolones are some examples of bactericidal antibiotics. A drug that disables bacteria by hindering growth and reproduction is called bacteriostatic. Tetracyclines, sulfonamides,

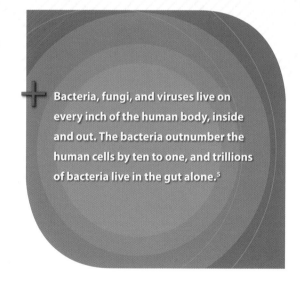

Bacteria, fungi, and viruses live on every inch of the human body, inside and out. The bacteria outnumber the human cells by ten to one, and trillions of bacteria live in the gut alone.[5]

The Body's Bacterial Defense System

The human body has several natural defenses against pathogenic bacteria. The skin serves as a wall against invaders. Many internal tissues are lined with cilia (tiny hairs) that block bacteria and foreign objects. Mucous membranes, such as those in the mouth and intestines, are coated with secretions that prevent bacteria from sticking. Some of these secretions contain antibacterial substances, such as the lysozyme in tears. If bacteria make it past these defenses, they face another defense system. Antibody proteins working for the immune system locate the invaders. These antibodies attract white blood cells to destroy the bacteria or escort the invaders to the spleen or lymph nodes for destruction.

and macrolides are some examples of bacteriostatic antibiotics. Bactericidal drugs usually act more quickly than bacteriostatic ones. Some antibiotics can be either bacteriostatic or bactericidal, depending on the dose or concentration. For example, metronidazole's bacteria-killing rate increases as dosage increases.

Antibiotics kill or slow pathogenic bacteria using different modes of action. Some antibiotics, such as penicillins, cephalosporins, bacitracin, and vancomycin, prevent bacteria from forming and maintaining their cell walls. Other antibiotics, such as polymyxin B and colistin, interfere with bacterial cell membranes. Other antibiotics, such as aminoglycosides, chloramphenicol, and tetracyclines, prevent bacteria from forming proteins. Bacteria are made largely of proteins; they cannot survive and multiply without forming proteins. Still other antibiotics, such as quinolones, metronidazole, and rifampin, slow the formation of genetic material, which must occur in order for bacteria to reproduce. Finally, some antibiotics, such as sulfonamides and trimethoprim, disrupt other cellular processes within bacteria so they can't function normally.

Finally, different antibiotics have different spectrums of activity. "Spectrum of activity" refers to how many species of bacteria an antibiotic affects. Antibiotics that affect only a limited group of bacteria are called narrow-spectrum antibiotics. For example, bacitracin affects only gram-positive bacteria, and aminoglycosides affect only aerobic bacteria. Antibiotics that affect a wide range of bacteria are called broad-spectrum antibiotics. For example, tetracyclines and fluoroquinolones affect both gram-positive and gram-negative bacteria.

Key Antibacterial Drug Classes

More than 150 antibiotics exist today.[6] But the number of antibiotics and their effects on specific bacteria are changing all the time. That is because bacteria and other microbes continue to evolve, and scientists continue to research them and develop antibiotics to fight them.

For these reasons, it is impossible to describe all antibacterial antibiotics—or to discuss any of them in great detail. It is, however, possible to explain the key classes in general terms.

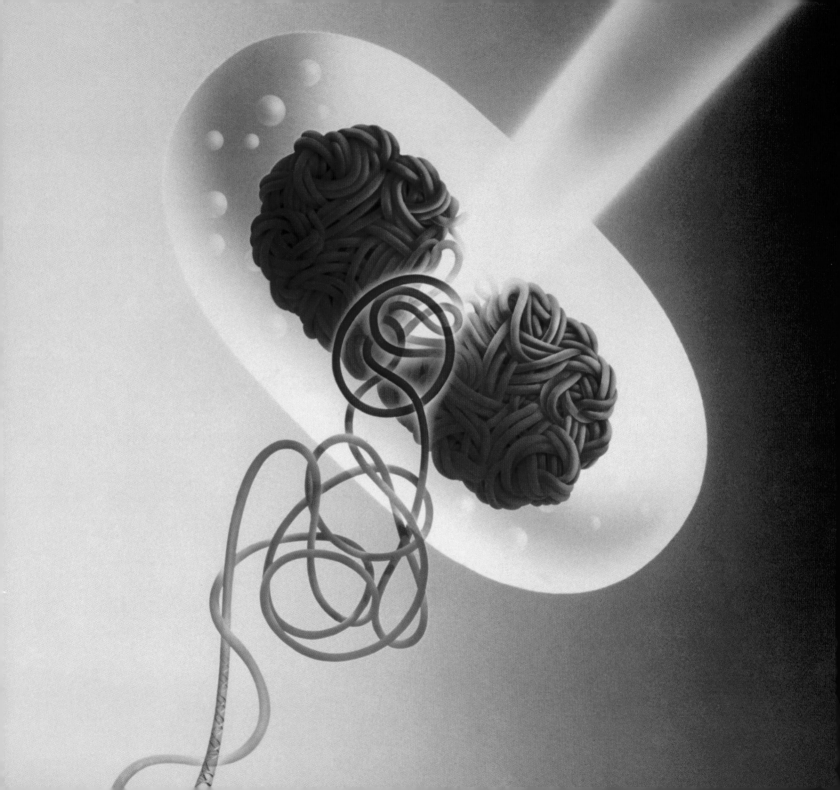

Penicillins

Penicillins are bactericidal. They kill bacteria by impairing the formation of cell walls.

Penicillins work against gram-positive bacteria, including several strains of staphylococci and streptococci, as well as *Enterococcus faecalis* (which causes meningitis and heart, blood, and urinary tract infections), and *Listeria monocytogenes* (which causes listeriosis, a food-borne infection). Penicillins also act against some gram-negative bacteria, such as *Escherichia coli* (food poisoning), *Haemophilus influenzae* (pneumonia, meningitis), *Neisseria gonorrhoeae* (gonorrhea), and *Treponema pallidum* (syphilis).

Most people tolerate penicillins well or have minor side effects. Digestive upset and diarrhea are common ones. Approximately 10 percent of patients have allergic reactions, which vary from a rash to anaphylaxis, a severe, whole-body allergic reaction.[7]

Cephalosporins

Similar to penicillins, cephalosporins are bactericidal. They kill bacteria by preventing them from forming cell walls.

All cephalosporins are broad-spectrum antibiotics. Cephalosporins belong to five different groups called generations. The different generations have somewhat different spectrums of activity. Some are

Antibiotics such as penicillin cause bacterial cell membranes to burst.

Allergic Reactions

When a person has an allergic reaction to an antibiotic, his or her immune system mistakenly recognizes the drug as a foreign invader. The body tries to get rid of the drug by producing large amounts of a chemical called histamine.

Histamine in the body causes symptoms that range from mild to severe. Mild to moderate symptoms include hives, skin rash, itchy skin or eyes, congestion, and swelling in the mouth and throat. Anaphylaxis is a severe, life-threatening reaction. It may include difficulty breathing, skin blueness, dizziness, fainting, anxiety, confusion, rapid pulse, nausea, diarrhea, and abdominal problems.

The antibiotic most likely to cause an allergic reaction is penicillin. Sulfa drug allergies are fairly common, too.

more active against gram-positive bacteria, while others work better against gram-negative bacteria.

The most common complaints are digestive upset, nausea, vomiting, and diarrhea. Only 1 to 3 percent of patients have allergic reactions, and life-threatening allergic reactions are rare.[8]

Carbapenems

Like penicillins and cephalosporins, carbapenems are bactericidal. They kill bacteria by interfering with cell wall formation.

Carbapenems are broad-spectrum antibiotics that are especially effective against gram-negative and anaerobic bacteria. They are often prescribed for resistant pathogens and serious infections in hospitalized patients. They are given intravenously. People do not usually react badly to carbapenems. Occasional side effects include

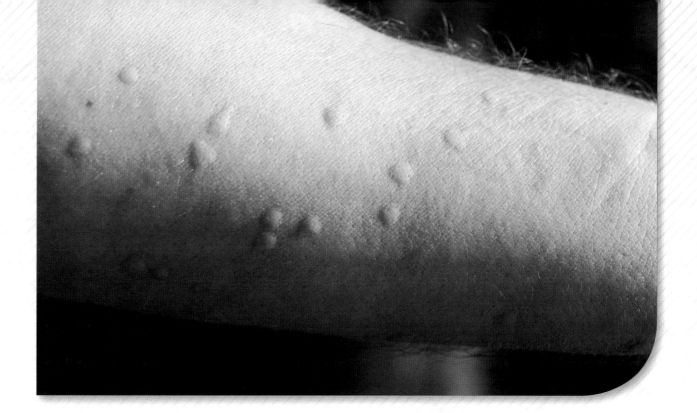

nausea and vomiting, elevated liver enzymes (which may indicate liver inflammation or damage), low white blood cell count (decreased disease-fighting cells), and seizures.

Monobactams

The monobactam class currently includes only one drug, aztreonam. Aztreonam is bactericidal. It kills bacteria by hindering cell wall formation.

Aztreonam is only active against gram-negative, aerobic bacteria. It is used to treat pneumonia, certain skin infections, urinary tract infections, and abdominal and pelvic infections caused by such bacteria. Many patients treated with aztreonam experience elevated liver enzymes and high white blood cell count. Less common reactions are rash, diarrhea, and nausea.

Aminoglycosides

Aminoglycosides are bactericidal antibiotics. They destroy bacteria by interfering with both protein and cell wall formation.

Aminoglycosides are primarily active against gram-negative, aerobic bacteria. They are often used to treat infections of the urinary tract, respiratory tract, skin, soft tissues, and blood caused by such bacteria.

Common side effects associated with aminoglycosides include kidney failure, balance problems, and hearing impairment. However, the effects usually go away when patients stop taking

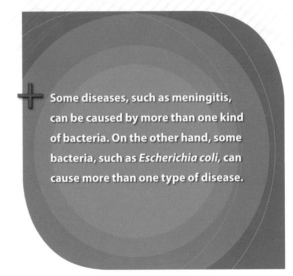

Some diseases, such as meningitis, can be caused by more than one kind of bacteria. On the other hand, some bacteria, such as *Escherichia coli*, can cause more than one type of disease.

the drug. Allergic reactions are not common but may include rash, fever, hives, swelling, and high white blood cell count.

Macrolides

Erythromycin was the first member of the macrolide class. It was discovered in 1952. Since then, scientists have developed semisynthetic versions of erythromycin (clarithromycin and azithromycin) and a related drug, telithromycin.

Macrolides are bacteriostatic. They disable bacteria by preventing protein formation. At high doses, macrolides may be bactericidal.

Macrolides are broad-spectrum antibiotics effective against gram-positive and gram-negative bacteria. They're often used for sinus infections, ear infections, strep throat, bronchitis, whooping cough, diphtheria, and pneumonia.

Common side effects include indigestion, abdominal cramps, diarrhea, nausea, vomiting, dizziness, and headaches. Rarer side effects are jaundice (yellow skin and eyes usually caused by liver problems), reversible hearing loss, tooth discoloration, anxiety, and blurred vision. Allergic reactions are rare.

Quinolones

Quinolones are bactericidal. They kill bacteria by preventing them from forming genetic material.

Quinolones act against many gram-negative bacteria. They are used for urinary tract infections, gonorrhea, pneumonia, sinus infections, soft tissue infections, and inflammation of the prostate gland. The quinolones ciprofloxacin and levofloxacin are used to treat anthrax.

The most common side effect is digestive upset. Less common side effects include headache, insomnia, dizziness, nerve pain, ruptured tendons, and elevated liver enzymes. Allergic reactions are rare but can be severe.

Sulfonamides

Most sulfonamides are bacteriostatic. They disable bacteria by interfering with cellular processes. One type of sulfonamide, silver sulfadiazine, is bactericidal. It destroys bacteria by preventing cell wall and cell membrane formation.

Sulfonamides are active against many gram-positive and gram-negative bacteria. They're often used for urinary tract infections, malaria, and toxoplasmosis. Toxoplasmosis, similar to malaria, is an infection caused by protozoans. Topical sulfonamides are used for burns.

Some Human Bacterial Diseases

Disease	Bacteria	Type
Anthrax	*Bacillus anthracis*	Gram-positive, rod-shaped
Botulism	*Clostridium botulinum*	Gram-positive, rod-shaped
Chlamydia	*Chlamydia trachomatis*	Gram-negative, spherical
Cholera	*Vibrio cholerae*	Gram-negative, comma-shaped
Dental caries	*Streptococcus mutans*	Gram-positive, spherical
Diphtheria	*Corynebacterium diphtheriae*	Gram-positive, rod- or club-shaped
Gonorrhea	*Neisseria gonorrhoeae*	Gram-negative, bean-shaped
Hansen's disease	*Mycobacterium leprae*	Gram-positive, rod-shaped
Lyme disease	*Borrelia burgdorferi*	Gram-positive, corkscrew-shaped
Peptic ulcers	*Helicobacter pylori*	Gram-negative, corkscrew-shaped
Plague	*Yersinia pestis*	Gram-negative, rod-shaped
Pneumonia	*Chlamydophila pneumoniae* *Mycoplasma pneumoniae* *Streptococcus pneumoniae*	Gram-negative, spherical or rod-shaped Gram-negative, variable shape Gram-positive, spherical
Tuberculosis	*Mycobacterium tuberculosis*	Gram-positive, rod-shaped
Typhoid fever	*Salmonella enterica typhi*	Gram-negative, rod-shaped
Typhus	*Rickettsia typhi*	Gram-negative, rod-shaped

Allergic reactions to sulfonamides, such as rashes and itching, are quite common. So are mild side effects such as nausea, vomiting, diarrhea, headache, and sensitivity to light. Severe reactions are rare.

Tetracyclines

Tetracyclines are bacteriostatic. They disable bacteria by hindering protein formation.

Tetracyclines have a very broad spectrum of activity. They affect gram-positive, gram-negative, aerobic, and anaerobic bacteria. They are especially useful against unusual bacteria. Doctors often prescribe tetracyclines for typhus, Rocky Mountain spotted fever, eye infections, infections of the urethra, and acne. They're also used against anthrax.

Collateral Damage

All antibiotics affect good bacteria as well as bad ones. When too many good bacteria die, it may result in overgrowth of fungus as well as a particularly resilient bacteria called *Clostridium difficile*. *C. difficile* is a serious complication with symptoms ranging from mild diarrhea to severe, life-threatening swelling of the large intestine.

Common side effects include digestive upset, nausea, vomiting, and diarrhea. Tetracyclines cause staining and deformed teeth in children. Sensitivity to light is a rarer side effect. Allergic reactions are not common.

Antifungal Antibiotics

When people are reading or talking about antibiotics, they usually think of bacteria, not fungi. But antibiotics can fight fungal infections, too. Such medicines are called antifungal antibiotics. How do antifungal antibiotics work? In order to understand that, one needs some basic knowledge about fungi.

Fungus Fundamentals

Fungi are very different from bacteria. Whereas all bacteria are single-celled organisms, fungi are not. They may be either single-celled or multicellular. Yeasts, for example, are single-celled fungi. Mushrooms and molds, however, are multicellular fungi.

Yeasts are single-celled fungi. When yeasts eat, the process is called fermentation, and it is necessary to make alcoholic beer and bread that rises.

The Fungi Forest

Fungi grow so fast that a single individual fungus can grow to be extremely large. One armillaria fungus growing in a Montana forest has an area of 37 acres (15 ha)! From the air, it looks like a huge light-colored patch of forest.

Most fungi are multicellular. In multicellular fungi, long chains of cells join end to end to form filaments, or threadlike structures, called hyphae. In larger fungi, such as mushrooms, the hyphae are packed together densely and are difficult to distinguish. Humans can barely make out hyphae with the naked eye.

All fungi obtain nutrients using a process called external digestion. They secrete enzymes into their surroundings. The enzymes break down the surrounding matter into a form the fungi can use for energy. Then the fungi absorb the broken-down matter back into their bodies.

Fungi can reproduce either asexually (on their own) or sexually (by joining with other fungi). Spores are a common means of asexual spreading. Spores are tiny, hardy little packets containing new individual fungus cells. They are dispersed by the wind and carried off by small animals. When spores land in a suitable environment, they start growing into new fungi.

Fungi are aggressive eaters and fast reproducers. When nutrients are plentiful and conditions are ideal, fungi can grow and spread very quickly. That's why it's not unusual to see a lawn full of mushrooms appear overnight. Scientists classify fungi into four groups based on their reproductive structures.

The Good and the Bad

Fungi do an important job in nature. Fungi and bacteria are Earth's main decomposers. They break down dead organisms and return their useful chemical compounds to the environment. Fungi are especially important for decomposing wood. They are the only type of organism that can break down lignin, a key component of wood.

Predatory Fungi

Some fungi are predatory. For example, if roundworms attack an oyster fungus, the fungus can secrete a chemical. The chemical drugs the roundworms trying to eat the fungus and then digests the roundworms. Other fungi can ensnare or fire projectiles at worms and other small animals.

Fungi also do many useful things for humans. They are necessary to make many products, such as bread, cheese, beer, wine, and other fermented drinks and foods. Some fungi, such as penicillium, produce antibacterial antibiotics. Other fungi convert pollutants in the environment into harmless substances. For example, at least three species of fungi have been used to remove excess selenium accumulated in the soil at the San Luis National Wildlife Refuge in California's San Joaquin Valley.

Helpful fungi are called nonpathogenic fungi. But fungi can be problematic, too. Unhelpful or disease-causing ones are called pathogenic fungi.

How Antibiotics Fight Fungi

The typical treatment for a fungal infection is medication with an antifungal antibiotic. The appropriate antibiotic depends on the type of fungus causing the infection.

As a rule, fungi are more complex than bacteria. In addition, fungal cells have more traits in common with the cells of mammals. For example, both fungi and mammals have the substance cholesterol in their cell membranes. A drug targeting any of those shared traits would damage both fungal and human cells. That means developing antifungal drugs is trickier than developing antibacterial ones. Antifungal antibiotics must target traits only fungi have.

So far, scientists have discovered three ways to destroy pathogenic fungi without destroying the human patient. One way is by targeting sterols, a group of chemical compounds that form inner cell walls in fungi. Most antifungal antibiotics use this method. A second way is by targeting the building blocks of outer fungal cell walls. These building blocks are chemical compounds called chitins, glucans, and mannoproteins. A third way is by interfering with genetic material inside a fungal cell.

Key Antifungal Drug Classes

Antifungal antibiotics are a much smaller group than antibacterial antibiotics. Antifungals fall into four main classes: polyenes, azoles, echinocandins, and pyrimidines.

Polyenes

Polyenes destroy the fungal cell membrane. Polyenes bind to sterols in the membrane. This creates holes in the membrane, causing the cell to leak and eventually die.

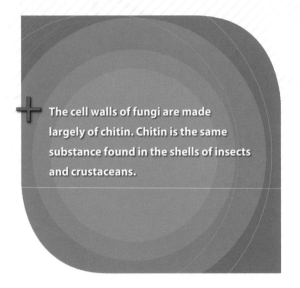

The cell walls of fungi are made largely of chitin. Chitin is the same substance found in the shells of insects and crustaceans.

Nystatin is a polyene antifungal that comes from the bacterium *Streptomyces noursei*. It treats fungal infections of the mouth, vagina, intestinal tract, and skin, such as diaper rash, jock itch, vaginal yeast infections, thrush, and athlete's foot. Patients can take nystatin by mouth or apply it to the skin. Its side effects may include itching, burning, rash, diarrhea, nausea, and stomach pain.

Another polyene antifungal is amphotericin B, a substance that comes from the bacterium *Streptomyces nodosus*. It is a strong drug usually reserved for serious fungal infections. It is given intravenously. It can cause many side effects, including fever, chills, nausea, vomiting, shortness of breath, wheezing, flushing, and muscle and joint pain.

Azoles

Azoles are synthetic drugs. They interfere with the formation of fungal cell membranes. They do this by stopping an enzyme necessary for producing sterols. When a fungus cannot produce sterols, it cannot form cell membranes, and it dies. Azoles also have some effect on certain protozoal infections.

The azoles include ketoconazole, fluconazole, itraconazole, voriconazole, and posaconazole, among others. Collectively, the azole drugs are effective against approximately 20 species of pathogenic yeasts, molds, and other fungi.[1] They are used for athlete's foot, ringworm, and vaginal yeast infections, as well as more serious infections.

Patients can take azoles by mouth, on the skin, or intravenously. Azoles have many side effects, but few are serious. Side effects usually occur with high doses of the drug. The most common azole side effects are nausea, vomiting, and diarrhea.

Echinocandins

Echinocandins are antifungal drugs that come from the fermentation of several different fungi. They interfere with cell wall formation by suppressing an enzyme necessary for forming glucans. When a fungus can't produce glucans, it can't form cell walls properly. The cell begins to leak, and it eventually breaks down and dies.

The echinocandin class includes the drugs caspofungin, micafungin, and anidulafungin. All echinocandins are given intravenously. They are active against approximately 12 pathogenic fungi.[2] Most patients tolerate echinocandins well. Side effects are rare and typically mild.

Pyrimidines

This class of antifungal drugs has one member: flucytosine. Flucytosine is the only antifungal antibiotic that kills fungi by interfering with the formation of genetic material. It is commonly used to treat fungal meningitis.

Flucytosine is taken by mouth. It is usually given together with amphotericin B. Its side effects include upset stomach, weakened immune system, and liver damage.

Some Human Fungal Diseases

Disease	Fungus	Symptoms
Aspergillosis	*Aspergillus fumigatus*	Wheezing, coughing, fever, chest pain, shortness of breath
Blastomycosis	*Blastomyces dermatitidis*	Cough, muscle aches, joint or chest pain, fever or chills
Candidiasis	*Candida albicans*	White patches in the mouth; genital itching, burning, or discharge; fever and chills
Coccidioidomycosis	*Coccidioides immitis*	Fever, cough, headache, upper-body rash, muscle aches, joint pain
Cryptococcosis	*Cryptococcus neoformans* *Cryptococcus gattii*	Shortness of breath, cough, fever, headache, chest pain, weight loss, lethargy
Fungal keratitis	*Fusarium verticillioides*	Eye pain, redness, discharge, blurred vision, sensitivity to light
Histoplasmosis	*Histoplasma capsulatum*	Fever, chest pains, dry cough, joint pain
Mucormycosis	*Mucoromycotina fungi*	Fever, headache, sinus pain, cough; blistered, red, black, or swollen skin
Pneumocystis pneumonia	*Pneumocystis jirovecii*	Fever, dry cough, shortness of breath, fatigue
Ringworm	*Trichophyton rubrum* *Trichophyton tonsurans* *Microsporum canis*	Skin itching, redness, scaling, cracking, ring-shaped rash, hair loss
Sporotrichosis	*Sporothrix schenckii*	Small painless skin bump that grows and multiplies

The Problem of Antibiotic Resistance

All microbes can develop antibiotic resistance. This means they can gain the ability to survive drugs meant to kill or disable them. The most dramatic examples of antibiotic resistance—and those that have the biggest impact on human health—occur among bacteria.

How Microbes Evolve to Survive

All traits in living things depend on genes. Genes are bits of the chemical code that living things contain. This chemical code tells cells how to make proteins, which are responsible for carrying out cellular activities. Each protein is coded by a particular gene. Each trait depends on a particular combination of genes. Traits that enable microbes to resist antibiotics are controlled by resistance genes.

Genes consist of DNA molecules that encode genetic information.

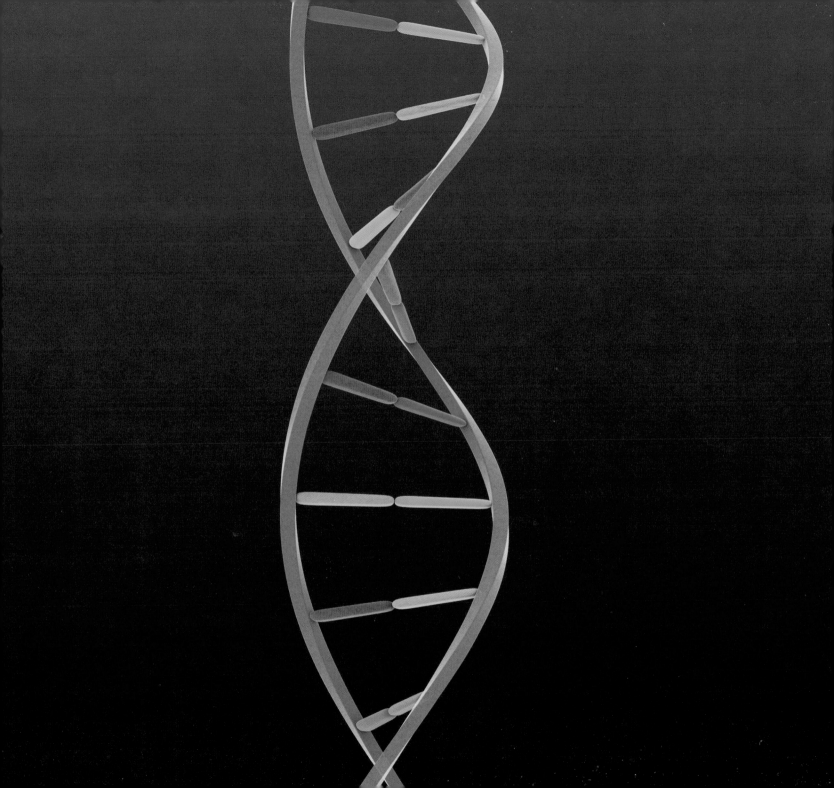

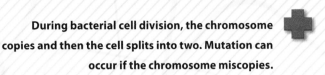

During bacterial cell division, the chromosome copies and then the cell splits into two. Mutation can occur if the chromosome miscopies.

Microbes gain the ability to evade antibiotics in two basic ways. One way is by mutating, or changing spontaneously, to gain resistance genes. When a microbe mutates, something miscopies during cell division, so the microbe forms with a mutation. A mutation is a trait that makes the microbe different in some way from other microbes of the same type. A mutation might give the microbe the ability to survive antibiotics.

Microbes can also acquire resistance genes from other microbes. This transfer can happen through direct contact, with the help of a virus, or by picking up stray genetic material from the environment.

When a population of microbes faces an antibiotic, the microbes that do not have resistance genes die. The microbes that do have resistance genes survive. They continue to grow and multiply. Each time the microbe population faces an antibiotic, the scenario repeats. As time goes by, the resistant microbes dominate the population. Eventually the drug doesn't work at all against that group of microbes.

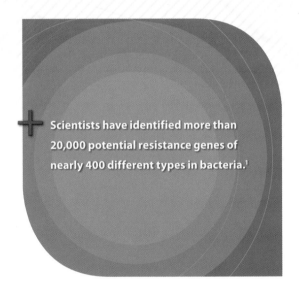

Scientists have identified more than 20,000 potential resistance genes of nearly 400 different types in bacteria.[1]

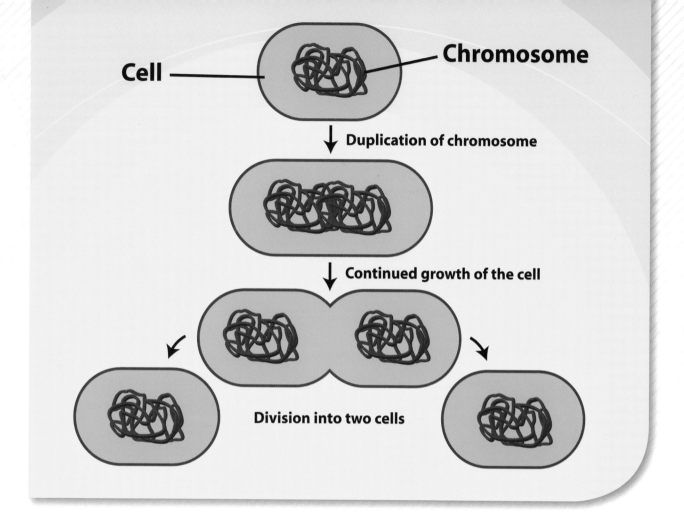

Resistance Mechanisms

Resistance genes enable microbes to fight back against antibiotics. Microbes fight back using four key mechanisms.

Microbes may use enzymes to break down or inactivate a drug. For example, a resistance gene enables some bacteria to produce penicillinase. Penicillinase is an enzyme that damages penicillin molecules. The damaged drug molecules have no effect on the bacteria.

Microbes can avoid accumulating a harmful amount of a drug. For example, a resistance gene may enable microbes to block uptake of a drug or to pump a drug out of the microbial cell once it gets in.

Microbes can prevent drugs from binding to microbial molecules. For example, a resistance gene allows some bacteria to prevent binding of the drug erythromycin.

Microbes can work around a drug intended to interfere with their metabolism. For example, some bacteria need to make a compound called folic acid in order to function. Sulfonamide prevents them from doing this. A resistance gene enables the bacteria to use folic acid from their environment instead of making it.

How People Encourage Antibiotic Resistance

Antibiotics have been around for approximately 70 years. During that time, people have gotten better and better at manufacturing antibiotics. They were difficult and expensive to make at first, but today manufacturing is relatively easy and cheap.

From Animals to Humans

Farmer Russ Kremer caught an antibiotic-resistant infection when he was gored by one of his boars. The drug-resistant bacteria passed to him from the boar. The bacteria had become resistant because the boars had been fed low doses of penicillin.

Thanks to this progress, over the decades humans have produced millions of tons of antibiotics and have used them in a wide variety of ways—sometimes for their intended purposes and sometimes not. People have used antibiotics as medicine not only for humans but also for animals. In addition, antibiotics are present in cleaning products, animal feed, and many other products.

At first glance, the proliferation of antibiotics may seem like a good thing. More antibiotics might seem to mean fewer microbes and better health. But this assumption is incorrect. As a result of human antibiotic use, the environment is now saturated with antibiotics. Antibiotic saturation helps microbe populations develop resistance to antibiotics. This happens because the more exposure microbes have to antibiotics, the more opportunities resistant microbes have to take over microbial populations.

People have a habit of overusing, underusing, and otherwise misusing antibiotics. Medicinal misuse is one key part of the problem, and it happens in a variety of ways. For example, the World Health Organization estimates approximately half the people who have bacterial pneumonia do not receive the correct antibiotics.[2] Many people who have viral infections demand—and receive—antibiotics from their doctors, even though antibiotics have no effect at all on viruses. Some people who receive an appropriate antibiotic prescription take it incorrectly. They stop taking the medicine once it has disabled enough pathogenic microbes to help them feel better instead of continuing the medicine until it has destroyed the whole population of microbes. Taking antibiotics for too short a time, for too long a time, at too low a dose, or for the wrong disease encourages microbe populations to develop resistance.

Misuse in animals is another big problem. Most antibiotics used in the United States are given to animals. In fact, approximately 70 percent of US antibiotics go to livestock such as cattle, chickens, and pigs.[3] And the antibiotics are not given only as medicine for disease; they are given essentially as food.

Low doses of antibiotics help farm animals grow faster. This means livestock farmers can produce more meat in less time, which helps them make more money. But unfortunately this practice also encourages microbe populations to develop antibiotic resistance. Many of the same microbes that live in and around livestock also live in and around humans, so resistance in livestock can lead to resistance in humans.

A third key way in which humans misuse antibiotics is by putting them in consumer products such as body soaps, sponges, detergents, and other products ranging from lip gloss to mattresses. There's no scientific evidence showing antibacterial products provide any benefit over traditional products. But there's plenty of evidence showing antibacterial products are harmful because they encourage microbe populations to become antibiotic resistant.

Viruses and Antivirals

Viruses are microscopic packets of genetic material encased in protein. They cannot grow and reproduce independently so they are not considered living organisms.

Although viruses aren't microbes like bacteria, fungi, and protozoans, viruses do cause disease. A virus does this by entering the cell of a host organism. The virus hijacks cellular processes to make copies of itself. When it makes enough copies, the host becomes sick and usually spreads the virus to another host. Viruses cause AIDS, chicken pox, Ebola, hepatitis B, herpes, influenza, measles, mononucleosis, mumps, pneumonia, polio, rabies, smallpox, and yellow fever, among other diseases.

Antibiotics do not work against viruses. A relatively small number of antiviral medications exist. These drugs try to prevent viruses from attaching or entering cells or from hijacking cellular processes. These drugs are somewhat toxic to humans because in order to damage viruses, the medications must also damage the host cells.

+ Traditional versus Antibacterial Products

Traditional cleaning products do their jobs quickly and then disappear. Soap, for example, loosens and lifts dirt, oil, and microbes from surfaces so water can rinse them away easily. Alcohol, bleach, and hydrogen peroxide destroy microbes swiftly and then evaporate.

Antibacterial products, by contrast, do not disappear. The antibiotics in them linger as residue. The residue continues to kill microbes—except the ones with resistance genes. It encourages vulnerable microbes to die off and resistant microbes to flourish.

Profile of the Problem

As of the 2010s, microbes have developed resistance mechanisms against all classes of antibiotics. In fact, many microbes are resistant to multiple drugs. These microbes are called multidrug-resistant (MDR) microbes. Several pathogenic microbes long linked to human disease epidemics, such as *Mycobacterium tuberculosis* (the tuberculosis bacterium), have evolved into MDR forms since the introduction of antibiotic drugs and consumer products.

MDR microbes that cause especially severe, dangerous, contagious, and hard-to-treat infections are called superbugs. The most notorious modern superbug is methicillin-resistant *Staphylococcus aureus*, or MRSA. *S. aureus* has been around for millennia and is well known as the culprit in common skin infections, such as boils. Penicillin controlled it for approximately a decade until it became penicillin resistant in the 1950s. Scientists then developed methicillin, which worked against *S. aureus* for approximately three years. This scenario has repeated many times, leading steadily to the development of MRSA. MRSA was once primarily a hospital problem, and therefore containable to some degree. But now it has moved into the general environment where anyone may pick it up at any time. This situation makes MRSA infections much harder to track, treat, and control.

Death rates due to infections caused by MDR microbes are high. As of 2010, approximately 25,000 people in the European Union were dying each year from such infections. The United States had even more deaths—more than 63,000 Americans per year were dying from hospital-acquired infections, which are usually caused by MDR microbes.[4] In the United States, 17,000 people die each year from MRSA alone.[5]

"Penicillin is . . . non-poisonous so there is no need to worry about giving an overdose and poisoning the patient. There may be a danger, though, in underdosage. It is not difficult to make microbes resistant to penicillin in the laboratory by exposing them to concentrations not sufficient to kill them.

". . . Mr. X has a sore throat. He buys some penicillin and gives himself, not enough to kill the streptococci but enough to educate them to resist penicillin. He then infects his wife. Mrs. X gets pneumonia and is treated with penicillin. As the streptococci are now resistant to penicillin the treatment fails. Mrs. X dies. Who is primarily responsible for Mrs. X's death? Why Mr. X, whose negligent use of penicillin changed the nature of the microbe. Moral: If you use penicillin, use enough."[6]

—*Alexander Fleming, Nobel Lecture, December 11, 1945*

As more and more microbes become resistant to more and more antibiotics, the need for new antibiotics grows. Meanwhile, drug companies grow less and less interested in developing new antibiotics. The cost of development is high, and there is no guarantee of turning a profit. Antibiotics begin losing market value as soon as they hit the market. They are all doomed to become obsolete sooner or later. As soon as people start using a new antibiotic, microbes start developing resistance to it. It is only a matter of time before any antibiotic becomes useless.

A perfect storm is brewing. Microbes are flourishing, while the arsenal of useful antibiotics is dwindling. While MRSA still responds to vancomycin, daptomycin, and linezolid antibiotics, it won't do so forever. Medical experts warn that humankind could soon return to a world in which they have little defense against infections.

MRSA and other infections are easy to pick up in
a hospital.

8

The Future of Antibiotics

The problem of antibiotic resistance is complex. Solving it will take effort from everyone —microbiologists, ecologists, health-care providers, educators, lawmakers, farm and drug industry workers, and the public.

Developing New Antibiotics

Eventually, all current antibiotics will become useless. If humans do not develop new antibiotic drugs, we will soon be virtually defenseless against pathogenic microbes. Few people welcome that prospect. So there's really only one choice: we must keep trying.

Researchers need to continue innovating new antibiotics to stay ahead of bacterial resistance.

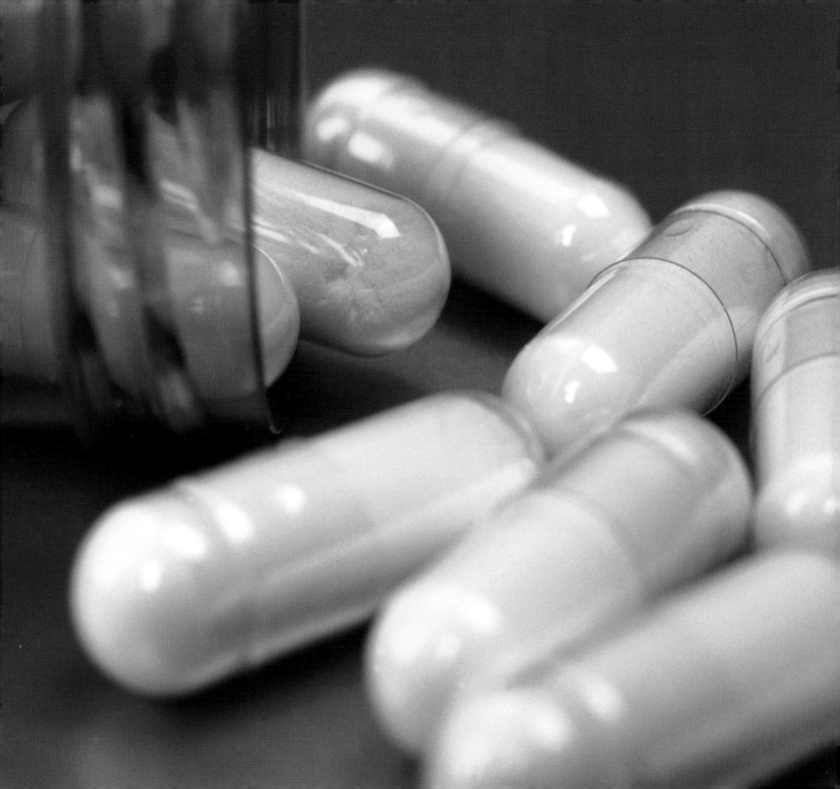

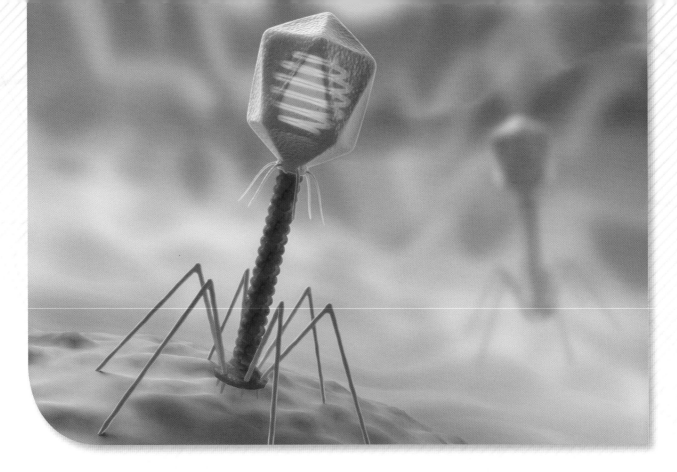

When antibiotic resistance first began to appear in the 1950s, scientists modified existing drugs to create new drugs. Through this approach, they developed many antibiotic derivatives that were less vulnerable to microbial resistance mechanisms. This approach still provides effective derivative drugs. But these, too, will eventually fall to antibiotic resistance. So it's important to try other strategies as well.

A bacteriophage virus attacks a bacteria.

Another approach is to continue exploring the ecological niches that have yielded many antibiotics. The most productive of these niches is soil, where scientists have discovered many species of antibiotic-secreting bacteria. However, modern exploration of this niche with the latest technology has been disappointing. It has not produced any new drug classes in more than 20 years.[1]

It is time to explore new niches. Some scientists are exploring Earth's waters instead of the soil. Other scientists are looking for antimicrobial compounds in the bodies of plants and animals. They are investigating bacteriophages, viruses that kill bacteria. Still other researchers are returning to the roots of antibiotic research. They are trying to develop completely synthetic antibiotics, like Salvarsan and sulfanilamide, by testing a wide variety of chemical compounds for antimicrobial activity.

Phage Therapy

Phage therapy is the use of bacteriophages to kill pathogenic bacteria. Bacteriophage means "bacteria eater." Bacteriophages are viruses that prey on bacteria. A phage attacks only a specific strain of bacteria. This means phage therapy can cure a patient's infection by destroying bad bacteria without harming the body's good bacteria, as broad-spectrum antibiotics do. Bacteria can develop phage resistance, but phages can mutate and evolve to fight phage-resistant bacteria.

Research shows phage therapy is effective in both animals and humans. Side effects are extremely rare. However, scientific and logistical challenges remain. Researchers still need to figure out a process for choosing the correct phage and ensuring it will stay in a patient's system long enough. And pharmaceutical companies must figure out how to manufacture and distribute phage products on a large scale.

The effort to develop synthetic antibiotics goes hand-in-hand with a search for new microbial targets. All current antibiotics target one of the following: microbial cell walls, cell membranes, proteins, genetic material, or metabolism. Some scientists are looking for different ways to destroy microbes. They hope to find smaller targets, such as specific molecules within microbes. They also hope to develop drugs that aim for multiple targets. Microbes would have a harder time developing resistance to these new types of antibiotics.

Developing new antibiotics requires not only an army of scientific minds to explore every possible avenue but also a great deal of public support. Antibiotics are inherently a losing proposition because they are expensive to develop and become useless so fast. Growing awareness about the problem of antibiotic resistance reduces the demand for antibiotics. Health-care providers are prescribing antibiotics less often. However, this means drug companies are making even less money on antibiotics and are therefore even less interested in developing new ones.

To address this challenge, the World Health Organization recommends governments offer drug companies incentives to encourage antibiotic research and development. It suggests public money should help pay for research and testing so drug companies will not lose money when they finally bring new antibiotics on the market.

Changing Our Ways

Developing new antibiotics is important, but it is only one part of solving the antibiotic crisis. If people hope to slow antibiotic resistance, they cannot go on using antibiotics at their current rate and in their current ways.

People can reduce the need for antibiotics—and therefore the development of antibiotic resistance—by working harder to prevent infection in the first place. Hand washing is one of the easiest and most effective ways people can protect themselves and others from microbial infections. People should wash their hands thoroughly before preparing or eating food, after coughing or sneezing, after changing a diaper, and after using the toilet. When soap and water aren't available, people can use an alcohol-based (not antibacterial) hand sanitizer instead. Humans can also avoid infection by getting vaccinated. Which vaccinations are appropriate depend on a person's age, medical history, and where the

The GAIN Act

On October 19, 2011, the US Senate introduced the Generating Antibiotic Incentives Now (GAIN) Act. This bill is designed to "spur development of new antibiotics to combat the spread of antibiotic resistant bacteria."[2] The bill was still in committee as of 2013.

However, another bill addressing antibiotic development has passed. President Barack Obama signed it into law on July 9, 2012. The FDA Safety and Innovation Act gives drug companies ten years—instead of the former five—to keep the data behind their products secret. Lawmakers hope this new law will keep competitors at bay for a longer time and motivate drug companies to bring new antibiotics to market.

Vaccines

Several bacterial diseases, such as diphtheria, whooping cough, and tetanus, are preventable with vaccines. A vaccine is a medication that allows a person to become immune to a disease without getting sick. Most vaccines guard against viral diseases.

After a person has a viral disease, the immune system makes antibodies against the virus. Antibodies are proteins that fight attacking microbes. If the virus attacks again, the immune system will remember it and send antibodies to fight off the infection. The person will not get sick this time because he or she is immune to that disease.

Vaccines are made from killed or weakened microbes. Vaccines are usually injections. Inside the body, a vaccine stimulates the immune system to make antibodies against a certain kind of microbe. If a vaccinated person is exposed to that microbe in the future, he or she most likely will not get sick.

patient lives or will travel to. Health-care providers and public health agencies can advise individuals on which vaccines they need. In addition, public health initiatives worldwide must make clean drinking water and proper sanitation accessible for everyone.

People must also use antibiotics properly as medicines. Antibiotic drugs should be available by prescription only, so their distribution and use can be better controlled. If a sick patient most likely has a virus, or the patient's infection is likely caused by an antibiotic-sensitive microbe, doctors should not prescribe antibiotics. When patients do receive antibiotics, they should be told why it is important they take the drugs exactly as instructed. Another way people can slow the development of antibiotic resistance is by avoiding antibacterial consumer products. They are no more effective than traditional products, and they make the problem worse.

Finally, nations that allow farmers to use antibiotics as livestock growth promoters should consider banning this practice. Some countries, such the Scandinavian nations and the Netherlands, have had success in slowing antibiotic resistance by setting strict guidelines for use. These guidelines include removing antibiotics from animal feed. In 2006, the entire European Union followed suit. Similar laws have not passed in the United States.

The Short and the Long of It

The antibiotic era has been short, compared with the long span of human history. But in that short time, humans have learned many important things about microbes. This knowledge has led to great advances in many areas of biology, medicine, and public health. For a while, humans have dominated microbes. People have also

+ Antibiotics without Prescription

Antibiotics are available without a prescription on the Internet, in developing nations around the world, and in some other countries, including some southern and eastern European nations. When people self-medicate, they often lack a correct diagnosis, the ability to choose the correct antibiotic, and knowledge of the treatment regimen. Thus, this use of antibiotics contributes to the problem of antibiotic resistance.

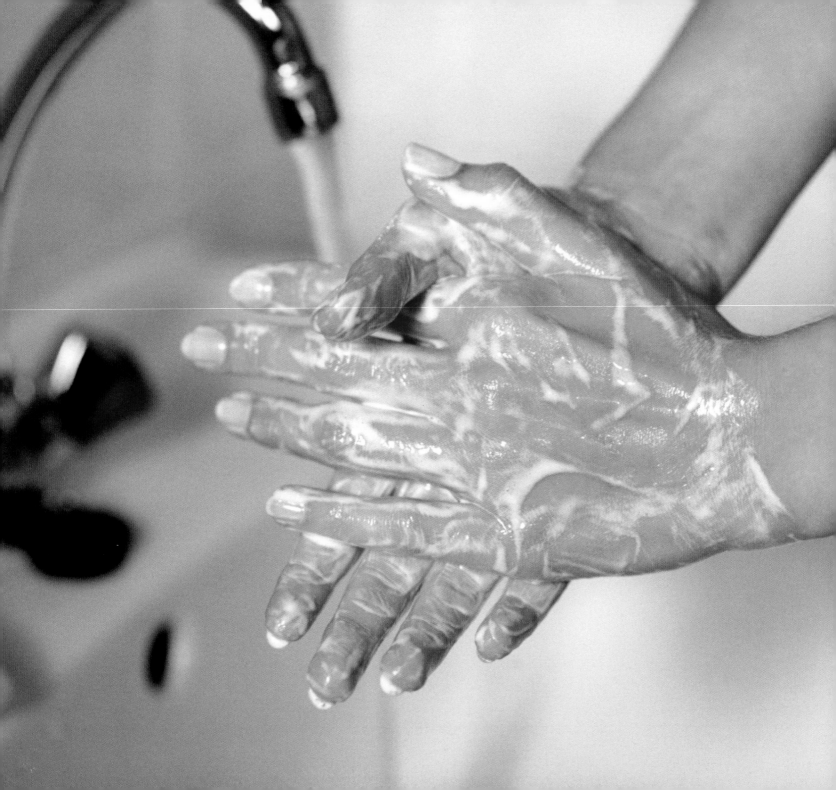

learned—just in time, we can hope—that microbes can and will overcome every human effort to destroy them.

People must not take antibiotics for granted. And they must realize that if they don't use them wisely and keep searching for new drugs, the end of the antibiotic era will arrive very soon.

"The world is on the brink of losing these miracle cures. . . . In the absence of urgent corrective and protective actions, the world is heading towards a post-antibiotic era, in which many common infections will no longer have a cure and, once again, kill unabated. . . . The responsibility for turning this situation around is entirely in our hands. . . . No action today means no cure tomorrow."[3]

—Margaret Chan, director-general of the World Health Organization, 2011

One of the best ways to prevent the spread of pathogenic bacteria isn't antibiotics—it's frequent hand washing with ordinary soap.

✚ Timeline

168 BCE

Chinese herbalists begin using the antimalarial plant artemisia to treat many illnesses.

100s–500s BCE

Ancient Nubians consume tetracycline-laced beer for good health and medicinal purposes.

1670s

Antonie van Leeuwenhoek is the first human to see microbes through a microscope.

1800s

French scientist Louis Pasteur and German scientist Robert Koch prove the germ theory of disease to be true.

1909

On his 606th try, German scientist Paul Ehrlich discovers a compound that cures syphilis in rabbits, leading to the development of the drug Salvarsan.

1943

Albert Schatz discovers the bacterium *Streptomyces griseus* produces a bactericidal substance, leading to the development of the antibiotic streptomycin.

1945

Giuseppe Brotzu discovers the fungus *Acremonium chrysogenum* produces a bactericidal substance, leading to the lengthy development of cephalosporin antibiotics.

1947

Paul Burkholder discovers the bacterium *Streptomyces venezuelae* produces an antibiotic substance, which becomes the first broad-spectrum antibiotic.

1950

Elizabeth Hazen and Rachel Brown discover a bacterium that produces a fungicidal substance, leading to the first antifungal antibiotic, nystatin.

1950

The first antibiotic-resistant bacteria appear.

1928

Alexander Fleming notices penicillium mold growing in a dish of bacteria have killed off the bacteria.

1935

Fleming gives up trying to develop penicillin; chemists in Germany and France discover the dye compound sulfanilamide can hinder bacterial growth.

1940

Howard Florey, Ernst Chain, and Norman Heatley successfully test penicillin in mice in May.

1941

Elva Akers is the first human to get an injection of penicillin, proving penicillin is safe for humans.

1941

Albert Alexander receives the first human penicillin treatment for a bacterial infection in February.

1970

Scientists develop the first fully synthetic antibiotics, trimethoprim and the fluoroquinolones.

1984

The popular antibiotic amoxicillin hits the market.

2011

The US Senate introduces the Generating Antibiotic Incentives Now (GAIN) Act on October 19.

2012

President Barack Obama signs the FDA Safety and Innovation Act into law on July 9.

2013

Microbes have developed resistance mechanisms against all classes of antibiotics.

Glossary

antibiotic resistance

The ability of microbes to survive drugs meant to kill or disable them.

antiseptic

A substance that slows or prevents the growth of microbes.

apothecary

Someone who prepares and sells medicines.

bacterium

A tiny one-celled organism that usually lives in colonies and works together for survival. Bacteria can be either beneficial or pathogenic.

enzyme

A protein that causes a specific chemical change in all parts of the body. All bodily functions, such as digestion and blood clotting, require enzymes. Enzymes exist in every organ and cell in the body.

fungus

A single-celled or multicellular organism; some include yeasts, mushrooms, and molds.

germ theory

The idea that microbes are the cause of many illnesses.

intravenously

Injected directly into the bloodstream through a vein.

metabolism

The process by which a living thing turns its food into energy.

microbe

A microscopic organism, such as a bacterium, fungus, or protozoan.

multidrug-resistant (MDR) microbe

A microbe that is resistant to multiple antibiotic drugs.

pathogenic

Disease causing.

pathology

The study of diseases.

protozoan

A single-celled organism that is more complex than bacteria.

resistance gene

A bit of chemical code within a microbe that enables it to fight back against antibiotics.

synthetic

Man-made, not naturally occurring. A semisynthetic substance is partially man-made.

Additional Resources

Selected Bibliography

Lax, Eric. *The Mold in Dr. Florey's Coat: The Story of the Penicillin Miracle.* New York: Henry Holt, 2004. Print.

Pringle, Peter. *Experiment Eleven: Dark Secrets behind the Discovery of a Wonder Drug.* New York: Walker, 2012. Print.

Spellberg, Brad. *Rising Plague: The Global Threat from Deadly Bacteria and Our Dwindling Arsenal to Fight Them.* New York: Prometheus, 2009. Print.

Further Readings

Klosterman, Lorrie. *Drug-Resistant Superbugs.* New York: Marshall Cavendish Benchmark, 2010. Print.

Murphy, Jim, and Alison Blank. *Invincible Microbe: Tuberculosis and the Never-Ending Search for a Cure.* Boston, MA: Clarion, 2012. Print.

Web Sites

To learn more about antibiotics, visit ABDO Publishing Company online at **www.abdopublishing.com**. Web sites about antibiotics are featured on our Book Links page. These links are routinely monitored and updated to provide the most current information available.

For More Information

Alliance for the Prudent Use of Antibiotics (APUA)

200 Harrison Avenue
Boston, MA 02111
617-636-0966
http://www.tufts.edu/med/apua

The APUA conducts research, education, and advocacy programs to control antimicrobial resistance and ensure access to effective antibiotics for current and future generations.

Pew Antibiotics and Innovation Project

Pew Health Group
901 E Street NW
Washington, DC 20004-2008
202-552-2000
http://www.pewhealth.org/projects/antibiotics-and-innovation-project-85899367216

The Pew Health Group's Antibiotics and Innovation Project develops and supports policies that will spur innovation of new antibiotics to fight infections today and to ensure a healthy nation in the future.

Source Notes

Chapter 1. Back from the Brink

1. Eric Lax. *The Mold in Dr. Florey's Coat: The Story of the Penicillin Miracle*. New York: Henry Holt, 2004. Print. 154.

2. Ibid. 154.

3. Fletcher, Charles. "First Clinical Use of Penicillin." *British Medical Journal* 289 (Dec. 1984): 1721. *PubMed*. Web. 12 Apr. 2013.

4. Eric Lax. *The Mold in Dr. Florey's Coat: The Story of the Penicillin Miracle*. New York: Henry Holt, 2004. Print. 155.

5. Jeremy Garwood. "Antibiotic Resistance: Who Will Win the Fight?" *Lab Times Online*. Lab Times Online, July 2011. Web. 12 Apr. 2013.

6. Eric Lax. *The Mold in Dr. Florey's Coat: The Story of the Penicillin Miracle*. New York: Henry Holt, 2004. Print. 14.

Chapter 2. Early Antimicrobials

1. "Leviticus 13:1–46 (New American Standard)." *BibleStudyTools.com*. Bible Study Tools, n.d. Web. 12 Apr. 2013.

2. "Leprosy." *A.D.A.M. Medical Encyclopedia*. PubMed Health, 24 Aug. 2011. Web. 12 Apr. 2013.

3. Eric Lax. *The Mold in Dr. Florey's Coat: The Story of the Penicillin Miracle*. New York: Henry Holt, 2004. Print. 24.

4. "Counting the Animalcules." *Lens on Leeuwenhoek*. Douglas Anderson, 1 Sep. 2009. Web. 12 Apr. 2013.

5. Ibid.

6. "Tiny Microscopes." *Lens on Leeuwenhoek*. Douglas Anderson, 1 Sep. 2009. Web. 12 Apr. 2013.

7. "Using the Microscopes." *Lens on Leeuwenhoek*. Lens on Leeuwenhoek. Douglas Anderson, 1 Sep. 2009. Web. 12 Apr. 2013.

8. Rustam I. Aminov. "A Brief History of the Antibiotic Era: Lessons Learned and Challenges for the Future." *Frontiers in Microbiology* 1 (8 Dec. 2010). *PubMed*. Web. 12 Apr. 2013.

9. "People and Discoveries: Alexander Fleming." *A Science Odyssey*. PBS/WGBH, 1998. Web. 12 Apr. 2013.

10. Rustam I. Aminov. "A Brief History of the Antibiotic Era: Lessons Learned and Challenges for the Future." *Frontiers in Microbiology* 1 (8 Dec. 2010). *PubMed*. Web. 12 Apr. 2013.

Chapter 3. Penicillin

1. Eric Lax. *The Mold in Dr. Florey's Coat: The Story of the Penicillin Miracle*. New York: Henry Holt, 2004. Print. 11.

2. Ibid. 79.

3. Ibid. 92.

4. Ibid. 123.

5. "The Story of Penicillin." *University of Oxford*. University of Oxford, 1 Jun. 2010. Web. 12 Apr. 2013.

6. Eric Lax. *The Mold in Dr. Florey's Coat: The Story of the Penicillin Miracle*. New York: Henry Holt, 2004. Print. 89.

7. Ibid. 152.

Chapter 4. Antibiotic Explosion

1. Stuart B. Levy. *The Antibiotic Paradox: How the Misuse of Antibiotics Destroys Their Curative Powers*. Cambridge, MA: Perseus, 2002. Print. 42.

2. Ibid. 45.

3. Peter Pringle. "Notebooks Shed Light on an Antibiotic's Contested Discovery." *New York Times*. New York Times, 11 Jun. 2012. Web. 12 Apr. 2013.

4. Stuart B. Levy. *The Antibiotic Paradox: How the Misuse of Antibiotics Destroys Their Curative Powers*. Cambridge, MA: Perseus, 2002. Print. 48.

5. Ibid. 50.

6. Ibid. 56.

Source Notes Continued

Chapter 5. Antibacterial Antibiotics

1. "Bacterial Infections." *MedLine Plus*. US National Library of Medicine, 26 Dec. 2012. Web. 12 Apr. 2013.

2. Ibid.

3. Ibid.

4. Stuart B. Levy. *The Antibiotic Paradox: How the Misuse of Antibiotics Destroys Their Curative Powers*. Cambridge, MA: Perseus, 2002. Print. 18.

5. Liz Szabo. "Our Microbes Are under Threat—and the Enemy Is Us." *USA Today*. USA Today, 18 Jul. 2012. Web. 9 Jan. 2013.

6. Jeremy Garwood. "Antibiotic Resistance: Who Will Win the Fight?" *Lab Times Online*. Lab Times Online, July 2011. Web. 12 Apr. 2013.

7. "957: Antibiotics Review." *NetCE: Continuing Education for Healthcare Professionals*. CME Resource, 2012. Web. 12 Apr. 2013.

8. Ibid.

Chapter 6. Antifungal Antibiotics

1. Paul O. Gubbins and Elias J. Anaissie. "Antifungal Therapy." *Clinical Mycology*. Ed. Elias J. Anaissie, Michael R. McGinnis, and Michael A. Pfaller. Philadelphia: Elsevier, 2009. 178. Web. 12 Apr. 2013.

2. Ibid. 182–183.

Chapter 7. The Problem of Antibiotic Resistance

1. Davies, Julian, and Dorothy Davies. "Origins and Evolution of Antibiotic Resistance." *Microbiology and Molecular Biology Reviews*. American Society for Microbiology, Sep. 2010. Web. 12 Apr. 2013.

2. Jeremy Garwood. "Antibiotic Resistance: Who Will Win the Fight?" *Lab Times Online*. Lab Times Online, July 2011. Web. 12 Apr. 2013.

3. Ibid.

4. Rustam I. Aminov. "A Brief History of the Antibiotic Era: Lessons Learned and Challenges for the Future." *Frontiers in Microbiology* 1 (8 Dec. 2010). *PubMed*. Web. 12 Apr. 2013.

5. Jeremy Garwood. "Antibiotic Resistance: Who Will Win the Fight?" *Lab Times Online*. Lab Times Online, July 2011. Web. 12 Apr. 2013.

6. Fleming, Alexander. "Nobel Lecture: Penicillin." *Nobelprize.org*. Nobel Media, 11 Dec. 1945. Web. 12 Apr. 2013.

Chapter 8. The Future of Antibiotics

1. Rustam I. Aminov. "A Brief History of the Antibiotic Era: Lessons Learned and Challenges for the Future." *Frontiers in Microbiology* 1 (8 Dec. 2010). *PubMed*. Web. 12 Apr. 2013.

2. Jeremy Garwood. "Antibiotic Resistance: Who Will Win the Fight?" *Lab Times Online*. Lab Times Online, July 2011. Web. 12 Apr. 2013.

3. Chan, Margaret. "Antimicrobial Resistance: No Action Today, No Cure Tomorrow." *World Health Organization*. World Health Organization, 7 Apr. 2011. Web. 12 Apr. 2013.

Index

+ About the Author

Christine Zuchora-Walske has been writing and editing books and articles for children, parents, and teachers for more than 20 years. Her author credits include books for children and young adults on science, history, and current events; books for adults on pregnancy and parenting; and more. Her book *Giant Octopuses* was an IRA Teacher's Choice book for 2001, and *Leaping Grasshoppers* was a 2001 NSTA/CBC Outstanding Science Trade Book for Students. Several of Christine's books have been well reviewed by *Horn Book* and *School Library Journal*. Christine lives in Minneapolis, Minnesota, with her husband and two children.

+ About the Consultant

Erika Ernst is an associate professor of pharmacy at the University of Iowa, College of Pharmacy, and a clinical pharmacy specialist at the University of Iowa, Hospitals and Clinics. She is a board-certified pharmacotherapy specialist with added qualifications in infectious diseases. Her research interests include the appropriate use of antimicrobial agents and antimicrobial resistance. Dr. Ernst has published widely in the area of infectious disease. She has authored numerous articles, including more than 50 scholarly papers and three book chapters, and is the editor of one book. Erika lives in Iowa City, Iowa, with her husband and three children.